JOURNEYS

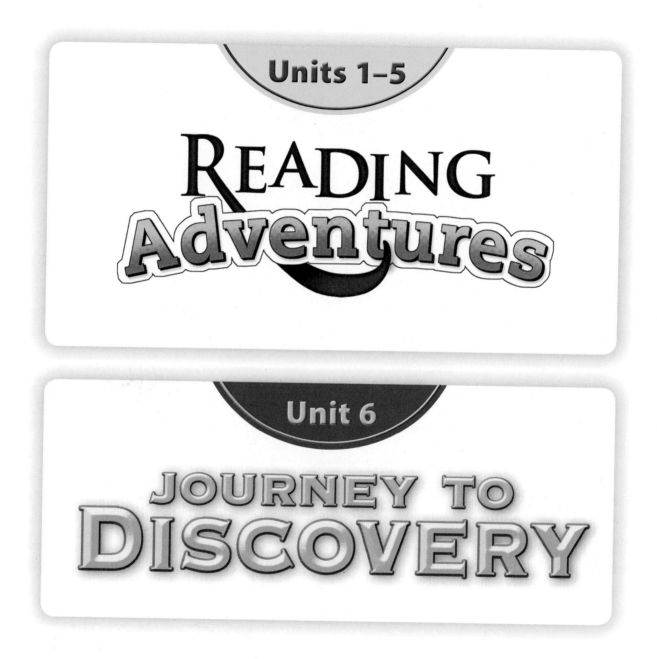

Units 1–5

READING Adventures

Unit 6

JOURNEY TO DISCOVERY

HOUGHTON MIFFLIN HARCOURT
School Publishers

Reading Adventures

The Multi-Tasker

by Becky Cheston   illustrated by Liz Callen

Chapter 1
It's a Cinch!

It was Sunday, and Ethan was in his room, multi-tasking. In his desk chair, he sat typing at the computer, where he had two other things going. One was a computer game and the other was e-mail, relegated to a little pop-up box in the right-hand corner of the screen, and that wasn't all. On his right, the television was tuned to a baseball game. Also, his favorite fantasy novel lay splayed open to Chapter 3—just in case of a lull.

A beep signaled the online arrival of his friend, Raymond. With a click, Ethan enlarged the message screen. *Hey, good news!* Raymond wrote. *The Y's going to let us use the gym on Tuesday and Thursday afternoons for our basketball clinic.* For social studies, Ethan's class was supposed to complete community service projects, and Raymond and he were planning to teach younger kids the basics of basketball.

Excellent! Ethan replied. *Hey, my phone's ringing. Bye for now.*

"Hi, Ethan? It's Kim, Kim Sasaki, from social studies class."

"Oh, Kim. Hi." Ethan sat up straight and felt a blush spread from his neck to his cheeks, warming his skin. "What's up?"

"Well," said Kim, "I was wondering if you wanted to sign up for my project. We're going to renovate the community center basement. You remember. It was damaged when it flooded last month."

"Well, sure," Ethan responded. Hanging out with Kim would be great, because she was really smart, energetic, and funny.

"Super!" said Kim. "We're meeting there on Tuesday at 3:30. See you then!"

The bedroom door squeaked open, but Ethan didn't turn around to see who was there. Instead, he checked the TV baseball score and moved on to the next level of the computer game.

"Wanna see what I'm wearing?" It was his little sister, Hannah, who was in kindergarten and seemed to change her clothes four times a day.

"Cool," said Ethan in a monotone voice as the computer keys clicked and the TV crowd cheered.

"You didn't even look!"

Ethan swiveled around in his chair, glanced at Hannah, and turned back to his game. "I hope you're not planning to go outside in that."

Belted around her middle, Hannah wore Ethan's old suit of armor, made from painted rubber. Around her neck was a feather boa in fluorescent pink, and dwarfing her head was his football helmet. Mercifully, she had left her feet bare, except for some nail polish—some of which had actually landed on her nails.

"It's for pre-TEND," said Hannah impatiently. "I'm not stupid, you know."

"Who are you supposed to be?" he asked.

"The sports fairy," Hannah said. "I'm the captain of the cheerleaders here to announce that lunch is ready." Then she flounced out of the room.

As Ethan swiveled to turn off his computer, a roar came from the television, where someone had just smacked a home run. A small voice began making noise in the back of his mind, asking, *Did Kim say to meet on Tuesday? Would he be getting out of basketball on time?* Well, he'd figure it out. Juggling two projects would be a cinch!

"Mmmm. Smells awesome!" Ethan said to himself as he raced down the stairs taking three steps at a time. His grandfather, a former chef, could whip up such delectable meals. "Yes!" Ethan shouted, spying the heaping dish of steaming pasta. "Homemade linguine!"

"It is not," said Hannah. "It's puz-*getti*."

"For your information," said Ethan, "*spaghetti* is long and round, while *linguine* is long and flat." He picked up a strand and dangled it at her. "Long and squirmy like an icky, squishy worm!"

"You don't scare me 'cuz I've got armor," said Hannah.

"The top of which you will remove at the table," exclaimed Ethan's mom as she reached for the football helmet.

"No!" shrieked Hannah, slapping her palms on top of her head.

"I don't have time for this, Little Missy, because in exactly one hour, I have to take sketches into the office." Their mom was a freelance graphic artist who worked long hours and had tight deadlines.

Grandpa, who was putting the finishing touches on the meal, paused briefly. "Diners always take their hats off at the chef's table!" he said and gently lifted the helmet off Hannah's head without drawing a protest. Once again, Grandpa's good nature and soothing presence calmed everyone's nerves.

Ethan hovered over the stove, eyeing the garlicky marinara sauce beckoning from a copper saucepan. He helped his grandfather put the food on the table and surveyed the meal. Besides the sauce, there was thick, crusty bread, a romaine lettuce salad, and freshly grated parmesan cheese in a glass shaker.

In his world, Ethan could sail smoothly back and forth from one task to another, but the kitchen was Grandpa's domain. Ethan admired the way Grandpa could juggle the ingredients of a multi-course meal and manage to serve everything—bread, pasta, sauce, salad—all at one time.

"I almost forgot," Ethan's mother said looking straight at him. "Remember, you have to pick up Hannah after school all this week because Grandpa's teaching that cooking seminar at the high school. We're counting on you."

"Isn't that great, Ethan?" Hannah beamed at him with a tomato-sauce smile.

"Yeah, great," he muttered. "Just great."

Chapter 2

After-School Activities

Excited by his plans for Tuesday afternoon, Ethan breezed through the school day with a bounce in his step. Then he remembered: He'd have Hannah with him again. Monday had been easy enough because he'd taken Hannah to the park and then, when they got home, she'd played in her room. He did get cajoled into playing Cinderella, but only once. But today was Tuesday.

After school, Ethan met Raymond at his locker. "You ready to head over there?" Raymond greeted him.

"Well, first I have to pick up Hannah," sighed Ethan.

"You mean she's coming with us?" said Raymond.

"Don't worry," said Ethan. "She won't be any trouble."

"Excuse me?" said Raymond, stopping in midstride. "This is your sister we're talking about, right?"

The boys headed for the kindergarten room, which was packed with people picking up their kids. They found Hannah there, waiting in her flowing pink and orange tutu, striped soccer jersey, and sparkly lavender high-top sneakers.

"Today, we're going to the Y to start our basketball clinic," began Ethan.

"But I want to go to the park!" cried Hannah, pouting.

Although the Y was only a fifteen-minute walk from school, Hannah's whining and dawdling doubled the time. Finally, with Ethan carrying Hannah piggyback style, they bounded up the steps to the Y. Inside, Ethan led the way down the hall and past the pool and locker rooms, energized by the familiar smells of chlorine, varnish, and sweaty sneakers.

A coach greeted them at the gym. "Hi, I'm Susan, and you boys must be Ethan and Raymond. You arrived just in time because here come the kids!" Wide-eyed second- and third-graders began piling into the gym, regarding Ethan and Raymond as if they were pros.

"Can I play?" asked Hannah.

Ethan smiled and looked at the coach. "That's my little sister," he said. Then he bent down and put his hands on Hannah's shoulders. "Listen, this clinic is for older kids. You don't even like basketball."

"I know!" she exclaimed. "I can be a cheerleader!"

"No!" Ethan said. The word came out a little too forcefully, so he softened his voice. "Look, you've got your coloring stuff, right? We're going to need a poster, so why don't you color a basketball picture for us?" He steered his sister to the sidelines and helped her get out her crayons and some paper.

Finally, he joined Raymond, who had already divided the kids into groups to start running drills. Ethan soon lost himself in the younger children's enthusiasm. He loved basketball: the feel of the ball under his palm, the squeak of sneakers on the polished wood floor, the swish of the net as a shot dropped in. No doubt about it, Ethan thought, playing basketball seemed more like a festive occasion than a sport.

Ethan was instructing the group on dribbling when something caught the corner of his eye—something pink and orange. Hannah was twirling her way across the gym floor.

"Hannah! You're not supposed to be out here!" Ethan grabbed her lightly, hoping no one had noticed her performance, but Raymond and the elementary children were looking over, laughing.

Smiling, Susan came to the rescue. "Why don't you let her play in my group."

"Thanks," said Ethan, returning to his group, but he found it difficult to focus. What embarrassing stunt would Hannah pull next?

After the forty-five-minute session, Ethan and Raymond passed out juice boxes and then waited until the last child had been picked up. Susan congratulated them, noting that they had run a successful opening clinic.

"Think about it," said Raymond, trying to twirl a ball on top of his finger. "This is for social studies. Every school project should be like this one!"

They took turns hoisting Hannah up to the basket so she could dunk the basketball. Then Ethan stopped suddenly, remembering.

"Oh, no. What time is it?" he shouted. The clock on the gymnasium wall read 3:35. "Come on, Hannah. Grab your stuff so we can go."

"What's up?" said Raymond. "I thought you were coming over to my house for a snack."

Ethan explained about his promise to Kim. "You mean you're doing two projects? Why would you—oh, I get it. Kim, right?"

"No, it's a very, very important project and . . ." Ethan started to protest.

"Sure, sure," said Raymond, laughing as he waved goodbye.

Ethan carried Hannah once again as he raced down the sidewalk. Upset about being dragged to another of Ethan's activities, Hannah began to whine in his ear. Ethan hardly noticed, though; he was concerned about what Kim would say when he finally showed up.

"Here we are!" Ethan said brightly to Hannah when they had reached the low red brick community center. Once an elementary school, the interior had been modernized, and now it boasted new activities rooms with computers and a kitchen. The basement, which had been damaged by the flooding, held a game room and a large function hall.

With her face creased by a frown, Kim waved wildly at Ethan. "Finally, Ethan. Can you come here and help us?" she shouted. She and Emily Powers were struggling outside the basement door with a stack of boxes filled with paint and supplies.

Ethan ran over. "Sorry I'm late, and sorry I have to baby-sit," he said, motioning toward Hannah.

"Where were you?" Kim asked. Ethan explained about the basketball clinic. Kim seemed surprised that both projects met on the same day. Maybe he should have mentioned it.

With Hannah following them in and out, Ethan apologized once more. As Kim recited everything that needed to be done, Ethan gave the scene a preliminary survey. The basement rooms were a mess. The flood had warped the floor and had left water stains on the walls. Plaster was peeling in spots. Ethan started shifting tables and chairs.

Suddenly, Hannah's bottom lip began to quiver. "I'm bored and tired and . . . , and I want to go home!" she whimpered, as tears filled her eyes and spilled down her cheeks.

Ethan sighed. His legs ached from basketball and from carrying Hannah everywhere. How was he going to tackle this second project? Here he was, the Multi-Tasker, adept at enjoying simultaneous activities and accomplishing his goals. What was happening to him?

"Hey. Looks like you've got your hands full," Kim said as she ruffled Hannah's hair. "You should probably take her home."

Apologizing yet again, Ethan picked up Hannah and headed out the door.

Chapter 3

Losing It

When he walked in the back door, Ethan was relieved to find Grandpa already home and in the kitchen, fixing a snack. Ethan slid into a chair with a sigh and asked, "How was your class, Grandpa?"

"Excellent," Grandpa replied. "We made zucchini bread with grated orange rind and chopped walnuts, and I brought a loaf home." He held out a plate with soft slices of brown bread, cheddar cheese, and purple grapes. Ethan and Hannah dove into the food eagerly. "And how was your afternoon?"

"It was yucky," said Hannah, still chomping, while crumbs spilled from the corners of her mouth. "We had to go a thousand, million places."

"A slight exaggeration," said Ethan wearily, yawning and stretching his arms over his head. "It was just two places: the Y and the community center."

"You look a little worn-out," Grandpa noted.

Ethan described what had happened. "I thought I could do both projects, but I guess I'm losing my touch."

"I don't know, kid," said Grandpa. "It's an awful lot to take on, especially with a little sister tagging along. Maybe you can prevail upon your mother to arrange some playdates for Hannah this week. There's her friend Molly . . ."

"Molly's not my friend anymore!" said Hannah. "But I'm planning to like her again tomorrow."

"I really let Kim down," said Ethan. "I'll be lucky if she even speaks to me again."

"Kim was bossy, and I didn't like her," said Hannah.

"She was not," said Ethan. "She had a big job to do."

"You smiled at her funny, and your ears turned red," Hannah reported, chuckling.

Ethan pushed back his chair indignantly. "Who asked for your opinion anyway?"

"Ahh, I see," said Grandpa.

"See what?" asked Ethan, embarrassed.

"See, Grandpa, look. His ears are doing it again!" said Hannah, pointing at Ethan and grinning.

"That's enough, Little Missy," said Grandpa. "Why don't you go to your room, put your backpack away, and change out of that tutu." When Hannah had gone, he turned to Ethan. "I bet you could devise a way to see this Kim person without overbooking yourself on her project. You know, you can take her out for a malt after school."

"Nobody does that anymore, Grandpa, but maybe—well, there's the spring dance." Then Ethan's shoulders slumped. He turned to Grandpa but couldn't keep eye contact. "I kind of feel like a failure."

"Nonsense!" said Grandpa, stirring a pot of soup. "If there's one thing I learned from my chef days, it's this: Never crowd the front of the stove. You can always put a few things on the back burner."

Slowly, Ethan returned to his room, reflecting on Grandpa's words. Then he plopped onto his bed. Opening his novel to Chapter 3, Ethan glanced around his room. From his desk, the computer beckoned, and wasn't "Sports Wrap-Up" on TV about now? He looked over, then shook his head. He'd see what it was like to do just this one thing—for at least ten minutes.

Look It Up

A dictionary or glossary is a great reference tool to use when you're reading *and* when you're writing. You can make sure that you understand the meaning of a word, that you use it correctly when you write, and that you pronounce and spell it correctly!

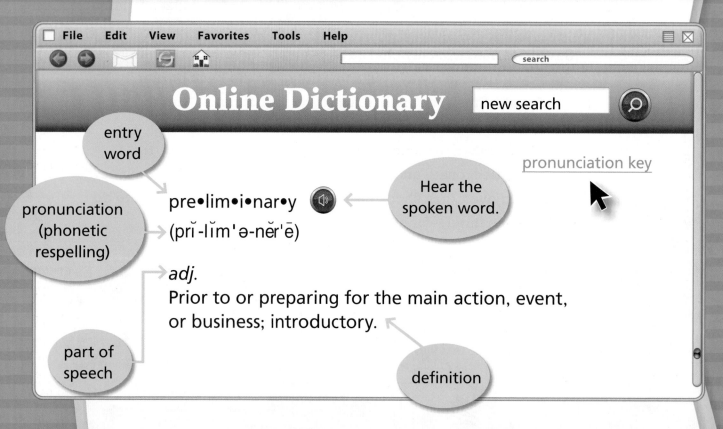

| File | Edit | View | Favorites | Tools | Help |

search

Online Dictionary
new search

entry word

pronunciation key

pre•lim•i•nar•y

Hear the spoken word.

pronunciation (phonetic respelling)
(prĭ-lĭm'ə-nĕr'ē)

adj.
Prior to or preparing for the main action, event, or business; introductory.

part of speech

definition

Use a digital dictionary or your **Student Book** glossary to find the pronunciation and meaning of the numbered words below. Make sure to identify the syllables with the primary stress. Then choose a word from the white box that rhymes with each stressed syllable.

1. persuade	2. gradually	3. identical	4. simulate
flea	pen	raid	pull
badge	purse	trim	rake

Answers: 1. raid 2. badge 3. pen 4. trim

What About ME?

Have you ever been part of a small-group discussion and wondered, *What about me? When will it be my turn to talk?*

Certainly, a good discussion calls for good communication! And that means group members should take care both to speak *and* to listen. In a good discussion, everyone should have a chance to contribute.

To get the most from a discussion, group members can carry out assigned roles. One member may keep track of time. Another may take notes on important ideas. It's also helpful if one student takes the role of the leader and makes sure that everyone gets a chance to speak *and* listen!

Speakers should
- express their ideas clearly
- build on each other's thoughts

Listeners should
- pay attention
- ask questions if something is unclear

Try This Out

Think about the many problems that Ethan created when he tried to multi-task. Also, consider the tasks and responsibilities that you must tackle in a week. Then decide when multi-tasking is acceptable and when it is best to focus on a single task.

Form small discussion groups. Then do the following:

1. Decide the roles that group members will take.
2. Discuss the issue thoroughly.
3. Create a general set of rules about multi-tasking.

Share and discuss your rules with classmates.

Don't Leave Them Hanging!

Good writers never leave their readers hanging! Their story conclusions follow naturally from the story events.

A good ending describes how a story problem is solved or how the story situation turns out. Often, a reader learns how the main character has changed. A good conclusion makes sense, is satisfying, and—maybe—makes the reader smile.

Think about the conclusion of "The Multi-Tasker."

> . . . Opening his novel to Chapter 3, Ethan glanced around his room. From his desk, the computer beckoned, and wasn't "Sports Wrap-Up" on TV about now?

If the story had ended there, you might have wondered, *Does Ethan go to his desk or turn on the TV? Has he learned a lesson?* The last two sentences answer those questions and show that Ethan is at least thinking about changing his ways.

> . . . He looked over, then shook his head. He'd see what it was like to do just this one thing—for at least ten minutes.

Good writers avoid endings that leave too many unanswered questions. They supply strong conclusions that tie story events together in satisfying ways.

How will my story end?

Reflect on Your Writing

Choose a story you have written in Unit 1, and review the conclusion. Ask yourself these questions:

Does my conclusion

☑ . . . tell how the story problem was resolved or how the main character changed?

☑ . . . answer any lingering questions the reader may have about what happened?

☑ . . . tie story events together in ways that satisfy the reader?

Improve your story by creating a strong, satisfying conclusion. Add details or revise what you have written to make your story ending even better!

NO LONGER LOST!

by Judy Schmauss

Just for a moment, let's go back in time. Imagine that you're living many, many, many years ago. You want to travel to a village far from your own. How will you know the right path to travel? How will you find your way home again?

You might look to the sky to find your answer. Why? The sun rises in the east and sets in the west. If you look at the night sky, you might be able to use the stars as a guide. The position of the sun and stars might give you some idea of where you need to go.

Fast-forward a few thousand years. Now as you travel, you have a new tool—a compass! Inside a compass is a free-floating needle. The end of the needle always points to the north. Now at least you know which way you're facing. Once you know that, you can figure out which way you need to go!

Now fast-forward again a few hundred years. You're planning a trip for next week. This time, modern technology will come to your rescue. You can find your way by using the Global Positioning System, more commonly known as GPS.

The GPS can tell you your exact location—and so much more. It will tell you how fast you're traveling and how far you've got to go until you reach your destination. It will even give you directions on how to get there.

The Global Positioning System was developed by the United States Department of Defense in the early 1970s. It was first used to keep track of military equipment out in the field. Now, however, you can find GPS units built into cars, airplanes, and cell phones. You can even buy a small GPS unit to plug into your car console or to carry around with you.

So just how does this system work? Let's take a look.

Sending Signals

The Global Positioning System is made up of a network of twenty-four satellites circling the globe more than 11,000 miles overhead. Every twelve hours, these solar-powered satellites orbit Earth. Because of the path that each satellite travels, at least four satellites can locate any site on Earth at any given time. Working together, the satellites transmit, or send out, regular signals. The signals tell their locations at the exact same time.

The satellite signals are picked up by a GPS receiver on Earth. The receiver figures out how far the signal from each satellite has traveled and the time it took for each signal to arrive.

Next, the GPS receiver combines the data from all the satellite signals. It uses a method called *trilateration* to tell you your location. This means that it calculates the distance between you, the satellites, and at least three known locations. This sounds complicated, but study the diagram on the next page to see how it works.

Satellite A puts you near Chicago, Illinois. You could be anywhere within this circle. Not so helpful if you're lost!

Then Satellite B figures out about how near you are to Detroit, Michigan. Combine this information, and you should be somewhere within the area where the circles overlap.

Next, Satellite C figures out how near you are to Milwaukee, Wisconsin. Now there will be *three* overlapping circles. The small place where the three circles meet shows where you are.

You are here!

Data from a fourth satellite results in a more precise location. To sum up, the GPS receiver can tell you where you are because it figures out the distances between you and four satellites.

GPS for Everyone

Once, GPS technology was used by only the military. Now, however, people are finding new uses for it daily. GPS technology has had a huge impact on our world. For example:

O A personal GPS unit in your car can tell you where you are, where you're going, how long it will take to get there, and even where to stop if you get hungry!

O With the use of GPS units, police, firefighters, and search-and-rescue teams can quickly get to the scene of an emergency.

O Scientists use GPS technology to study animals around the globe. Endangered animals can be tracked and monitored, giving scientists important information about ways to protect them.

O In addition, ships at sea use GPS technology to identify their exact locations, as well as to navigate shallow waters and harbors safely.

O GPS technology gives scientists tools to measure changes to the earth's surface. These changes may signal the possibility of an earthquake or a volcanic eruption.

O Companies also use GPS technology to track their shipments. They can tell where their goods are at any point in time and even let you know when the delivery truck has arrived at your door!

Directions Made Easy

Many people use GPS technology to get accurate directions for driving from one place to another.

Just a few years ago, people had to rely on paper maps or atlases to find their way to new locations. However, maps and atlases become outdated quickly, and they don't always provide detailed information about smaller roads or detours. Because the information stored inside GPS units can be updated, you can now get accurate, easy-to-follow directions to find your way.

Let's say that you're visiting an unfamiliar city and want to find the Slugger Baseball Museum. When you type in the address—1234 Diamond Street—your GPS unit will figure out exactly where you are. Then it will give step-by-step directions that show the streets to take and the turns to make to get to the museum. Should you take a wrong turn or miss a road, the GPS unit will figure out your new location and give you new directions.

Search and Rescue

Additional uses for GPS technology have been developed. For example, GPS devices combined with other technology can help reunite lost pets with their owners.

Remember that a GPS unit only receives, or picks up, signals from the satellites in order to pinpoint a location. To be helpful, though, the unit must pass along that information, too. A transmitter that sends out a signal is also needed.

How does this work? A tiny transmitter is combined with a GPS receiver on a special tag or collar. The receiver identifies the pet's location. Then the transmitter sends a signal with that data to the nearest cell tower or station. The data gets passed along to other towers or stations until it reaches the pet's owner. Now the animal's location and direction of travel can be used to help recover it.

In much the same way, GPS technology can be used in search-and-rescue missions. After a hurricane, an earthquake, or some other natural disaster, recognizable signs and landmarks may be destroyed. Using GPS devices along with other equipment, rescuers can identify locations quickly. They then transmit that information to guide emergency workers to the spot where they are needed. Emergency workers can also identify the areas that were already searched. This saves time and resources—and sometimes lives!

Animal Tracking

Some scientists track animals in order to learn more about a creature's habits, range, and behavior.

Look at the chart below. A bird species called the Franklin's Gull was tracked in order to learn about its migrating habits. Scientists discovered that these amazing birds may migrate 5,000 miles each spring and 5,000 miles again each fall!

The Franklin's Gull has an average flying speed of about 30 miles per hour. It flies for an average of 12 hours a day.

Day	Miles
1	360
2	720
3	1,080
4	1,440
5	1,800
6	2,160
7	2,520

According to this chart, it would take the birds about two weeks to fly from Canada to South America.

So, how do scientists collect this useful and fascinating information?

At one time, this meant locating the animals that scientists wanted to study and then following right behind them to see where they went or catching them later. Collecting accurate information about birds and water creatures was especially difficult!

More recently, scientists tracked animals by placing radio bands or tags on them. Since radio signals only travel short distances, scientists still had to follow the animals closely or predict where they might go. In some cases, the scientists had to wait to hear from people who had found a tagged animal to record its location.

GPS technology has changed all that. Once a transmitter is placed on an animal, scientists can check on its exact whereabouts at any given time, even from far away. In a study using a GPS transmitter to monitor zebras in a large herd, one scientist remarked, "It was way cool to see the location and movements of many individuals from the data downloaded from only one!"

Marine Navigation

The oceans of the world cover almost seventy percent of the surface of our planet. With thousands of miles of empty sea and no landmarks, how do ships and other marine vessels find their way?

Long ago, seafarers used the position of the sun and stars to guide them. With the invention of the compass and other instruments—along with more detailed maps and charts—sailors had better ways of navigating the vast open waters of the ocean. But there were still uncertainties when storms hit and blew the ships off course. Heavy cloud cover and thick fog also caused major problems for ships at sea.

Today, ocean travel is faster, easier, and safer due to the use of the Global Positioning System. Ships with GPS receivers can pinpoint their exact position anywhere on the vast, empty ocean. And now, GPS technology works with special marine software that links the GPS satellite signals to radar and depth finders. Sent to a ship's onboard instruments, the GPS information helps ships navigate safely along rocky coasts and in shallow waters.

New Uses

Used now on land, sea, and air, GPS technology has improved steadily in the last thirty years. With each new improvement, people continue to find new and surprising ways to use GPS.

Today, some large grocery chains and department stores use GPS technology to help shoppers locate the items they need! Photographers now have digital cameras equipped with GPS receivers that identify the place where a photo is snapped. They can also give a bird's-eye view of the site. Likewise, an outdoor treasure-hunt game that makes use of GPS technology is growing in popularity.

What new ways will people use GPS technology in the future? Could GPS technology one day help find lost homework? Will a similar system be set up to help us explore Mars or another planet?

There's no doubt that the Global Positioning System—with its satellites, computers, and portable units—is here to stay. We are a society that seems to be constantly on the move. With GPS technology, we can always be sure to find our way home again!

DID YOU KNOW ?

- The amount of power used to transmit a GPS satellite signal is the same as the power in a 50-watt light bulb.

- The GPS satellites are only 24 of the existing 2,500 satellites that orbit Earth at an altitude of over 11,000 miles.

- Each satellite weighs about 2,000 pounds, which is the weight of an average elephant.

- Each satellite is built to last about 10 years. For that reason, replacements are always being built and launched into space.

Don't Be Confused

Quick—tell me the meaning of *console*!

You can't tell the meaning unless you see how the homograph *console* is used in a sentence.

> My mom's new car has a GPS built into the front **console** just below the radio.
>
> After my friend got lost on our hiking trip, I had to **console** and comfort her.

A homograph isn't really confusing! Just be sure to use the context clues, or the other words in the sentence, to figure out the intended meaning of the word.

What's the intended meaning of each of the homographs in this sentence?

> The softball **pitcher** accidentally hit the glass **pitcher** on the refreshment table.

For each homograph below, write a sentence with context clues. Leave a blank line where the homograph should be. Trade papers with a partner, and take turns identifying the correct homograph and its meaning. Tell which context clues helped you to figure it out!

Homographs		
content	squash	squall
might	bound	strain

Suppose researchers asked 100 people how they would use a personal GPS device. The researchers could report on what they learned by using words, quotes, and examples—or they could present the survey results in a clear and highly visual way.

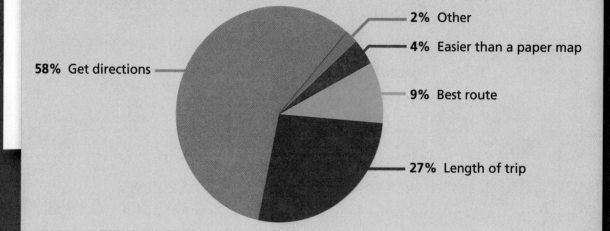

Reasons for Using a Personal GPS Device

2% Other

4% Easier than a paper map

9% Best route

58% Get directions

27% Length of trip

A pie chart is one way to organize numerical data, such as the survey results above. Note how the title of the chart identifies the information being displayed. The chart itself gives an instant overview of the survey results. Each colored "slice" of the "pie" stands for one group of the survey participants. The percentages connected to the colored slices provide the details.

To summarize the information in the chart, briefly explain its purpose. Then tell how the percentages, or details, explain information about the topic of the chart.

With a partner, discuss the chart on page RA29 of the Student Magazine, and take turns summarizing what it shows. Then share your summaries with the rest of the class.

Let Me Show You the Way!

When you write to inform or persuade, don't let your readers get lost! Make your thinking clear by supplying the right information.

- Include facts, examples, and specific vocabulary words related to your topic.

- Supply definitions if you think a word or concept is unfamiliar to your readers.

- Consider adding quotes from experts to support your ideas.

Which of these sentences gives the reader a clearer understanding of how a GPS device works?

> This big thing that goes around Earth sends out some kind of beeping to a box.

> A satellite that orbits, or travels around, Earth sends out a signal to a GPS unit.

One way to keep your writing on track is to make a word web like the one below. Then you can refer to the concepts, ideas, and terms on your web as you write.

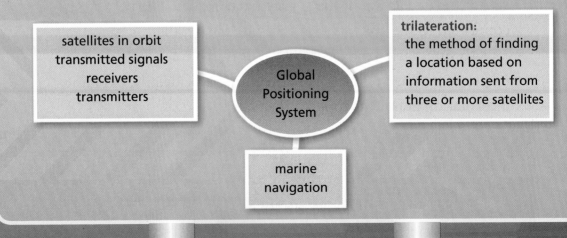

satellites in orbit
transmitted signals
receivers
transmitters

Global Positioning System

trilateration:
the method of finding a location based on information sent from three or more satellites

marine navigation

Reflect on Your Writing

Choose a piece of your writing that informs or explains. Find ways to revise it to keep your readers on the right track. Think about

- replacing vague phrases with specific, topic-related vocabulary words

- adding quotes from experts about your topic

- supplying definitions for words your readers may not know

Once you've finished making your revisions, read your work again. This time, your message should come in loud and clear!

Tea Time!

by Lawrence Tolbert

Why Toss Tea?

On November 29, 1773, a handbill, or flyer, was posted all over Boston. It stated,

Friends! Brethren! Countrymen! That worst of Plagues, the detested tea, shipped for this port by the East India Company, is now arrived in the harbor....

The flyer called for the colonists of Massachusetts to unite and protest the importing of this tea. Weeks later, on the evening of December 16, 1773, the water in Boston Harbor became one giant pot of tea as the revolt against King George and the British government took place. In just a few short hours, colonists tossed 90,000 pounds of tea overboard. This famous event would later become known as the Boston Tea Party.

The Boston Tea Party took place on December 16, 1773.

Send It Back!

So, just what led to this wasteful tossing of perfectly good tea?

Taxes! That's what led to this famous event in history. In 1767 the British government passed laws giving its country the right to tax American colonies. The colonies protested that, with no one to represent them in England, they had no say in how they were being governed, what items were to be taxed, and how the tax money would be spent. In the end, the British government dropped all the taxes, except for the one on tea— the beloved drink of British people and American colonists alike.

Drinking tea was a custom that had traveled to the new land with the American colonists. Even before the Boston Tea Party, the stiff taxes placed on tea by the British government led many colonists to boycott tea altogether.

However, King George III was certain that the colonists could not hold to their boycotts and tea replacements for long. He continued to send ships filled with tea, and he expected the colonists to pay the required taxes.

King George III ruled Britain during the time of the Boston Tea Party.

When three ships filled with tea arrived in Boston around early December 1773, the colonists had finally had enough and refused to pay the tax. They called for the tea to be sent back. Town meetings were called to "devise measures for getting rid of this annoyance," according to Samuel Cooper, a Boston Tea Party participant.

Despite repeated requests, Governor Hutchinson of the Massachusetts Bay Colony refused to send the tea back to England. Instead, he insisted that the tea be unloaded and the taxes paid by midnight, December 16th. If not, he would force the unloading of the tea with the use of warships and cannons. To prove his point, he ordered two ships to stand guard at the entrance to Boston Harbor. No ships could leave the harbor without his permission.

Town meetings were called to decide what should be done with the tea being held onboard three ships in the harbor.

Many of the more outspoken Bostonians felt that the governor's refusal to send the tea back to England left them few options.

On December 16, 1773, Samuel Adams, a leader known for organizing protests against the British government, announced to those at a special town meeting, "This meeting can do no more to save the country." Were his words a signal that the time had come for action?

A group of men at the meeting hollered and whooped a war cry. Then they marched down to Griffin's Wharf in disguise. Hundreds of onlookers followed to watch events unfold.

Samuel Adams encouraged his fellow colonists to protest the tax on tea.

That Fateful Night

Joshua Wyeth, age 16, was one of many to march upon the wharf. He described his experience to a journalist many years later:

> I had but a few hours warning of what was intended to be done. To prevent discovery we agreed to wear ragged clothes . . . , dressing to resemble Indians. Our most intimate friends among the spectators had not the least knowledge of us.
>
> At the appointed time, we met in an old building at the head of the wharf, and fell in one after another, as if by accident, so as not to excite suspicion . . . .
>
> We boarded the ship moored by the wharf, and our leader ordered the captain and crew to open the hatchways, and hand us the hoisting tackle and rope, assuring them that no harm was intended them. . . . Some of our number then jumped into the hold, and passed the chests to the tackle. As they were hauled on deck others knocked them open with axes, and others raised them to the railing and discharged their contents overboard. All who were not needed on this ship went on board the others, where the same ceremonies were repeated.
>
> We were merry, in an undertone, at the idea of making so large a cup of tea for the fishes, but [we used] no more words than were absolutely necessary. . . . I never worked harder in my life.

Accounts vary as to just how many colonists took part in the "ceremonies."

Quietly and swiftly, the chests of tea were dumped into the harbor.

George Hewes, a Boston shoemaker, also joined in. Over fifty years after the event, Hewes recalled that night:

It was now evening, and I immediately dressed myself in the costume of an Indian, equipped with a small hatchet, . . . and a club. After having painted my face and hands with coal dust in the shop of a blacksmith, I repaired to Griffin's wharf, where the ships lay that contained the tea.

When I first appeared in the street after being thus disguised, I fell in with many who were dressed, equipped and painted as I was, and who fell in with me, and marched in order to the place of our destination.

When we arrived at the wharf, there were three of our number who assumed an authority to direct our operations, to which we readily submitted. They divided us into three parties, for the purpose of boarding the three ships which contained the tea at the same time. The name of him who commanded the division to which I was assigned was Leonard Pitt. The names of the other commanders I never knew.

Once aboard the ships, the colonists demanded that the ships' captains hand over the keys to the hatches, or compartments, where the tea was stored. The chests of tea were hauled on deck and split open with tomahawks. The contents were then dumped overboard. Tea leaves scattered across the water. As Hewes recalls,

> *In about three hours from the time we went on board, we had thus broken and thrown overboard every tea chest to be found in the ship, while those in the other ships were disposing of the tea in the same way at the same time. We were surrounded by British armed ships, but no attempt was made to resist us.*

The following day, tea leaves could still be seen floating in the harbor. Colonists in rowboats beat the tea with their paddles until they were certain the tea would be of no use for drinking.

Caught in the Act

Several accounts describe how a few citizens quietly attempted to save some tea for their own use. With hopes that no one was looking, they filled their coat pockets with the precious leaves. However, their deeds were soon discovered and their pockets emptied of the tea. With a few swift kicks as punishment, these citizens were sent on their way!

Standing Up to the King

Despite the pounds of tea destroyed on the evening of December 16, 1773, the disguised colonists did no other damage to the ships or the people aboard them. Overall, it was a peaceful protest meant to send a strong message to King George and the British government.

Here is how Hewes recalled the conclusion to the event:

> *We then quietly retired to our several places of residence, without having any conversation with each other, or taking any measures to discover who were our associates; nor do I recollect of our having had the knowledge of the name of a single individual concerned in that affair, except that of Leonard Pitt. There appeared to be an understanding that each individual should volunteer his services, keep his own secret, and risk the consequences for himself.*

For many days after the historic protest, the streets of Boston were quiet and orderly.

The days and nights that followed this event were quiet in Boston. If for only a short time, the colonists had spoken out against British rule. Eventually, King George ordered punishment for his disobedient subjects, leading the colonies one step closer to revolution!

Speak the King's English

> *Friends! Brethren! Countrymen! That worst of Plagues, the detested tea, shipped for this port by the East India Company, is now arrived in the harbor. . . .*

If you had lived in Boston in 1773, you probably would have had little trouble understanding this flyer.

Yet today, a word like *brethren* sounds strange to our ears, and the order of the words seems odd. That is because the version of English spoken by the colonists, as well as the speech patterns they used, were much different from the way we speak today.

The colonists also would have used a formal register, or style of speaking, more often than we do today. In modern times, we generally use an informal register, or casual style, in familiar settings.

With a partner, talk about the meaning of the message on the flyer above and the young colonist's words to the right. Then, together, rewrite the message and the colonist's words in modern English.

> I had but a few hours warning of what was intended to be done.

Words, Alive!

In 1860, Henry Wadsworth Longfellow published "The Midnight Ride of Paul Revere." Today, with the variety of media available, you can experience the poem in exciting new ways that Longfellow never could have imagined.

If you were a filmmaker, how might you make the poem come alive? Which forms of media best capture the spirit, thrill, and suspense of Longfellow's stirring words: artwork, a video, dramatic music, or something else?

SET THE MOOD

With a partner, plan a multimedia presentation of the poem to share with your classmates.

- Together, review the poem. Highlight words and phrases that lend themselves to dramatic interpretation or that express mood.

- Now mark your copies of the poem. Identify lines or stanzas where visuals, music, or other sound effects might contribute more to the meaning, tone, or mood you want to capture.

Don't Forget to Signal

On the open sea, ships have long used flags to signal and communicate with other ships. Good writers also use signals to communicate well with their readers.

In opinion pieces, a writer uses signal words to connect his or her opinion with the reasons for that opinion. Signal words help readers follow the thinking process of the writer.

Similarly, it is important to bring an opinion piece to a close with a strong conclusion. You've explained the reasons why you hold a particular opinion. Now restate that opinion and summarize your reasons. Leave no doubt in the reader's mind about where you stand!

Which of these conclusions clearly signals the writer's opinion?

Signal Words

consequently

specifically

especially

for example

The men who destroyed the tea took a big risk. They were very brave.

In the end, the brave men who destroyed the tea took a big risk. They specifically chose to ignore the armed ships that could have attacked them at any time.

Reflect on Your Writing

Look back at a piece of your writing that expresses an opinion. Will your reader know how to navigate through your opinion to your reasons? Does the reader know when you're coming to the end? Are your signals clear? Ask yourself questions.

Have I . . .

▶ used words and phrases to signal links between my opinion and the reasons for that opinion?

▶ concluded with a strong statement that restates my opinion and sums up the reasons I used to support my opinion?

Send a clear message to your readers! Add signal words and strengthen your conclusion.

A Royal Mystery

by Audrey Carangelo   illustrated by Jessica Secheret

Camp Katahdin, a summer camp for girls and boys from seven to twelve years old, is located deep in the woods and far from any towns or cities. There are miles of nature trails, horseback riding and jumping arenas, and a wide, deep lake.

CHARACTERS:

• Misty • Althea • Rena • Narrator • Julio • Gerard

Scene I

Setting: A tent platform at Camp Katahdin

Misty: Althea! Good to see you back at camp.

Althea: You too, Misty! Hope you don't mind that I have a new tentmate this year.

Misty: *(laughing)* No problemo! I'm sorry for being such a klutz last year! I probably cost you the trophy. I think I had problems with just about every event!

Althea: We can't all be good at everything! I'm hoping my new roomie will know how to ride a horse, unlike someone I know.

Misty: *(a little offended)* Hey, canoe-tipping doesn't help tentmates win a tournament either.

Althea: *(sheepishly)* Oh, yeah, I sort of forgot about that.

Misty: So, where is your new tentmate?

Althea: I guess she's not here yet. Keep your fingers crossed that she's not scared of horses!

Rena: *(stepping into the tent, lugging two heavy suitcases)* Good day! Good day!

Althea: Hey! Welcome, tentmate!

Rena: *(tossing matching leather luggage onto a cot)* Umph! Gerard has packed these so heavily! And I've had to carry them myself!

Misty: *(whispering and rolling her eyes)* Uh, oh! Fancy matching luggage? That's not a good sign—but never judge a book by its cover, right?

Althea: *(eyeing the new girl warily)* Hi, I'm Althea. That's a lot of stuff there.

Misty: And I'm Misty, Althea's tentmate from last year.

Rena: Wonderful to meet you both! My name is Rena. *(looking around the tent, confused)* May I ask where the closets might be?

Althea: *(pointing to an army trunk)* You're looking at it! You ride horses?

Rena: Certainly. I'm a champion jumper. And where is the bed? I don't see one.

Althea: *(pointing to a cot)* So you can ride! Any other sports?

Rena: I've won a few archery contests. And, excuse me, . . . restrooms?

Althea: *(nodding toward the open tent flap)* Next to the showers. Impressive, Rena. I think we'll get along fine! Come on, it's time for lunch. To the mess tent!

Rena: The what?

Misty: Mess tent. It's where we eat.

Rena: Where we eat? Are you quite certain?

Althea: *(teasing and mimicking Rena's tone)* Yes. Quite.

(The girls exit, with Rena holding the flap back gingerly as she steps through.)

Setting: Later that evening at the entrance of the girls' tent

Narrator: The girls return to the tent, struggling under the weight of several mattresses.

Rena: I can't thank you enough for locating these extra mattresses.

Althea: *(swinging the mattresses)* No prob. Let's swing them up there. One, two, three—heave!

Rena: Earlier, I tried out that silly cot. It filled me with such discomfort that I'm sure I will never be able to fall asleep.

Althea: Don't worry. Lots of campers grab extra mattresses the first night.

Rena: Really?

Althea: Well, not six—but still.

Rena: Would you like one?

Althea: Nah, I'm good. Let's try and get some sleep now. We need to be on our game tomorrow. A perfect bull's-eye every time, right? *(shooting an imaginary bow)*

Scene III

Setting: A few days later, inside the girls' tent

Narrator: Rena is trying to adjust to camp life, as both girls get to know each other better.

Rena: *(entering the tent)* Ohhhh. I do so hate camping! The showers are absolutely primitive.

Althea: *(laughing)* That's all part of camping, right?

Rena: I wouldn't know.

Althea: I don't get why you're here, Rena. You don't seem like a summer camp kind of girl.

Rena: *(shrugging her shoulders)* I suppose you're right. This was Gerard's idea. He believes that I should meet more young people my age.

Althea: Who's Gerard?

Rena: He's . . . just Gerard. That's all. *(seeing Althea's frustration)* Well, fine then. Gerard is my temporary guardian. My parents are away for a bit, and I miss them terribly. There! Are you happy?

Althea: Whoa. Sorry, Rena. I didn't mean to upset you.

Rena: I would prefer not to talk about it. *(pauses)* So, why don't you show me more of the camp? I'd like to see those horse stables now.

Scene IV

Setting: Later the same day in the interior of a horse stable

Narrator: Inside the cool stable, it smells of horses and fresh hay. Sunlight filters through a row of windows as the girls visit Charger, Althea's favorite horse.

Rena: *(stepping inside and looking around)* It's so peaceful here. *(excitedly)* Oh, what a beautiful Appaloosa! I love their spotted markings, don't you?

Althea: I thought you'd like Charger. He's really smart, and just wait 'til you ride him! So, do you get to ride much where you're from? Where *are* you from anyway?

Rena: A city in the North.

Althea: New York? Boston?

Rena: *(interrupting)* . . . the North*west*.

Althea: Seattle? Vancouver? You're Canadian! Yeah, that makes sense with your strange accent.

Rena: Accent?

Althea: Yeah, like now. *(mimicking Rena)* Whatever do you mean by accent? *(seeing Rena's irritation)* Sorry. So, where'd you say you're from?

Rena: We move frequently. *(She looks uncomfortable.)*

Althea: Fine. Changing subject now! So, are you really a champion horse jumper?

Rena: I've been riding almost my entire life. I suppose I have quite a few trophies.

Althea: *(Her eyes light up.)* You know of the Tournament of Champions, right?

Rena: No, I've never heard of it. *(teasing)* Only every day since I stepped into the tent!

Althea: Funny. So, listen, we can get a higher team score if *you* jump Charger. I'll enter the softball throw instead.

Rena: I would be honored to jump Charger. And don't worry, Althea, I vow to help you win that trophy this year.

Althea: Super! But for now, we've won the honor of mucking out the horse stalls. *(handing Rena a pitchfork)*

Rena: Excuse me? Did you say *muck* out? *(sputtering)* Please say you're joking! What's that odor?

Althea: Just part of camping!

Setting: Early morning in the last week of summer camp

Narrator: The campers are preparing for the day's tournament events. Althea rests on her cot, reading a book of fairy tales.

Althea: *(to herself)* That's it! Now I know why Rena is being so secretive.

Rena: *(entering the tent)* Is that right? First of all, I don't have secrets. I simply choose not to share certain things.

Althea: Sorry. I didn't mean to offend you. I'm just trying to figure you out.

Rena: Figure *me* out? *(angrily)* Perhaps you should figure yourself out! For example, why is it so important for you to win some silly trophy? Oh, dear! Forgive me for shouting. That was very rude.

Althea: You weren't exactly shouting.

Rena: I must run now. *(picking up a towel)* I promised that I would take swimming lessons, but now I'm late.

Althea: Wait, Rena. I know you hate swimming and that you're only taking lessons because you said you'd help me win.

Rena: Well, I also hate breaking promises. *(looking hurt)* I must ask, though, what do you mean, help *you* win? Have I made the mistake of assuming that we are a team?

(Rena exits.)

Fairy
Tales

Setting: In the girls' tent later that same morning

Narrator: Rena walks into the tent still wearing her swimming cap. Althea looks up from her reading. She's still immersed in the book of fairy tales.

Althea: Enjoy the lake?

Rena: Lake? Is that what you call that dreadful little mudhole? As soon as I change, I'm going to saddle Charger and practice jumping. Would you care to come?

Althea: Yeah, but I have the canoe race this afternoon. I'm resting up for the big competition.

Rena: Althea! I nearly forgot. I'm so happy you reminded me. Of course, I'll be there for your race. We shall win this tournament *together*.

Althea: *(her face lights up)* Really? I thought you still might be angry. You told me to figure myself out and . . .

Rena: *(interrupting)* And have you figured yourself out?

Althea: I think so.

Rena: Well, I'm ready to listen.

Althea: Okay, so I don't have anything that I'm good at back home. Here, I'm good at stuff—well, except canoeing. If I take home the camp trophy, then I can remember I'm good at something, even when I'm not here. Does that make any sense?

Rena: It makes perfect sense. And you thought of all that while I was swimming? *(teasing)* There may be hope for you after all. (sneezing) Achoo! I knew that nasty water was five degrees too—*ACHOO!*—chilly.

Althea: *(throwing a pillow)* Toughen up, girl! We have a tournament to win!

Scene VII

Setting: The lake at Camp Katahdin

Narrator: The canoe race is under way. The shore is lined with cheering campers. Julio, a camp counselor, is announcing the race.

Julio: *(excitedly)* It's a close race, campers! Althea is holding on to second place! Oh, no! She bungled the turn! Althea slips back to fourth. Wait—here comes Misty, now pulling into second place!

Rena: Go, Althea!

Julio: Althea's digging those paddles in! She's neck and neck with Kara. Wait! Kara has dropped back and Althea has moved into third place!

(The crowd on the beach shouts as the canoes race toward the finish line.)

Rena: You can do it, Althea!

Julio: What a race! At the finish line, it's Jai in first place! Misty takes second, and by a matter of inches, Althea has placed third! Great job, everyone!

(Rena runs to congratulate Althea.)

Rena: You did it!

Althea: Did what? I didn't win the race.

Rena: Well, you did your best, and that's what counts. We can still win the tournament.

Althea: *(glumly)* Yeah, but . . .

Rena: Absolutely no *buts*! You told me the same thing when I placed third at the track meet.

Althea: *(brightening)* We got a good lead when you earned the top jumping score with Charger.

Rena: And your winning softball throw added several points!

Althea: *(excitedly)* So, if we place first and second in the archery contest tomorrow, we could still win the tournament!

Rena: Your competitiveness is certainly contagious!

Althea: Last one to the mess tent gets stable duty!

Rena: *(laughing)* I adore how you make everything a contest!

Scene VIII

Setting: Evening in the girls' tent

Narrator: Tomorrow is the last day of camp and the last day of the tournament. Althea is determined to solve the mystery that surrounds Rena. She has pocketed a few peanuts from the mess tent.

(Althea slips one peanut beneath Rena's six mattresses.)

Rena: *(entering the tent holding her toothbrush)* I'm terribly excited about tomorrow! I may not sleep at all!

Althea: Same here. But the sooner we sleep, the sooner we win! So, lights out!

Narrator: Rena tosses and turns in her bunk all night. Meanwhile, Althea stays awake to see if Rena falls asleep. Morning arrives at last.

Rena: OWWWW! I feel as if I've slept on top of a boulder the size of Mount Rushmore.

Althea: Yes! It worked!

Rena: What worked?

(Althea digs under Rena's mattresses until she finds what she is looking for—a peanut.)

Althea: *(brandishing the peanut)* This! This worked. I put it under your mattress last night, and you felt it! You felt this tiny peanut through *six* mattresses.

Rena: I don't understand. Why would you want to torture me in such a way?

Althea: Torture? I'm investigating a mystery! I'm trying to get to the bottom of, well, I'm . . .

Rena: Torturing me.

Althea: Okay, well, sorry about that part. But you'll be really happy to learn what I found out.

Rena: *(sarcastically)* Happy? Oh, wonderful! Please, tell me. *(rubbing her sore leg)* What did you find out?

Althea: Well, m'lady, this peanut—this insignificant legume—proves beyond a shadow of a doubt, that you are a descendant of kings and queens! Royalty! I'm talking a *princess*!

Rena: A *princess*? Whatever do you mean?

Althea: It's all right here. Listen *(reading from the book)*:

. . . those of royal blood are sensitive to the slightest chills and faintest odors. They speak with formality and refinement. Their sensitivity is such that they may detect a tiny pea below twenty mattresses. In these ways and more, royalty and their descendants are different from the common population.

Rena: Are you saying . . . ?

Althea: Think about it. Stinky stables. Chilly lake. The way you speak, and now the peanut!

Rena: *(musing)* Could this be true? And if so, then what shall I do?

Althea: What you shall do is join me on the battlefield so we can win the tournament!

Rena: Althea, look at this bruise! I can't compete with such an injury!

Althea: Nonsense! A princess must rise above a mere bruise. So, get a move on!

(Both girls exit.)

Scene IX

Setting: Later that day, on a wooded trail leading from the archery field to the girls' tent

Narrator: Rena and Althea carry the trophy, struggling under its enormous weight.

Rena: The bull's-eye you shot was positively amazing!

Althea: Well, Princess, your last arrow split *my* arrow in half— that's *royally* amazing!

Narrator: Before the girls reach their tent, Rena spots Gerard standing near a limousine.

Rena: Gerard! Come and meet Althea.

Gerard: *(smiling and eyeing the trophy)* Brava, Miss Rena! But now, I must deliver a message that I believe you'll find quite important. *(handing her a small envelope)*

Narrator: Rena reads the note.

Rena: *(reading)* "Darling Rena, we regret that you have heard from us so infrequently of late. Much has happened in our tiny kingdom of Corelia. Quite recently, your father and I were named to succeed your great-uncle as rulers. It is time for us all to be together again. Gerard will accompany you on your journey. We count the hours until you arrive."

Narrator: Rena pulls a necklace from the envelope. From a chain hangs a golden disk imprinted with a regal lion.

Althea: *(looking puzzled)* Hey, look at this! *(pulling a delicate gold chain from her shirt)* My aunt sent this to me when I was five. . . .

Rena: Oh, my. Then this means . . . ?

Gerard: *(looking at his watch)* Ladies, a plane awaits! This conversation must continue at another time.

Rena: *(laughing)* Goodbye, Princess!

Althea: Goodbye yourself! I better see you here next year. I'll have solved another royal mystery by then!

THE END

WORDS TO LIVE BY

"Never judge a book by its cover!"

What did Misty mean when she whispered that to Althea in Scene I of "A Royal Mystery"? Has anyone ever said that to you?

You might have wondered, *What does that mean? We've been talking about a person, not a book.*

This proverb has been quoted often over the years, and it still seems true. By looking at a book cover, you can't tell what's written on the inside pages. Similarly, you can't tell what a person is like just from his or her appearance.

Proverbs are short, clever phrases that originated from old folk wisdom. That's why the words used to express them may sound a little strange to our modern ears. The wisdom of the proverbs still holds true, though. In fact, after many generations, people still remember and repeat these familiar sayings!

On a separate piece of paper, match the meaning on the left with its proverb on the right. You may want to keep track in your notebook of any proverbs and other common sayings you hear and read.

1. There's no point in being upset over something that has already happened.

a. A problem shared is a problem halved.

2. Take advantage of a favorable situation while you have the chance.

b. It's no use crying over spilt milk.

3. If you want something very much, you will find a way to get it.

c. Make hay while the sun shines.

4. You can get things done faster and easier if you work together.

d. Where there's a will there's a way.

In a group, take turns describing instances when one of these proverbs was true for you.

You Be the JUDGE

In the drama "A Royal Mystery," Rena spoke very formally while Althea's speech was more informal. Imagine being at camp with Rena and she greets you:

> *It is a pleasure to meet you this fine day!*

You could answer formally: *It's a pleasure to meet you, as well!* Or you might answer her informally: *Yeah, good to meet you too.*

Use formal language in speaking situations where you want to make a good impression. Use correct grammar and appropriate language, and avoid using slang or casual expressions that you might use with friends and family.

JUDGE THE SITUATION

Some of the situations below call for formal speech. In others, informal speech would be perfectly acceptable. Discuss each with a friend, and decide how you would adapt your speech to fit the situation.

1. Asking the principal's permission to use the gym for a science project fair

2. Making plans with friends to see a new movie

3. Approaching a neighbor about hiring you to walk his dog

WAKE UP!

Snooooooze....snooooooze....snoooooze

If you've ever fallen asleep watching a movie, seeing a play, or reading a book, then it's very likely the pacing of the story was off.

Good writers don't want to bore you. They want to excite you and keep you in suspense. To do this, writers unveil story events at differing rates by using a technique called pacing. Writers skim over routine events and activities, giving just a few details, to focus your attention on the important moments in their stories.

To highlight the important scenes, writers expand them by providing lots of details—exciting action, vivid descriptions, and lively dialogue. Changing the pacing of story events helps writers create excitement and suspense so their stories come alive.

Think about the scene in "A Royal Mystery" in which Althea explains why she hid the peanut under Rena's mattresses.

→ Suspense builds as Althea hides the peanut, the girls spend a sleepless night, and Althea reveals her scheme the next morning.

→ Critical details about Rena's discomfort and Althea's motives come to light through the snappy dialogue between the girls.

Then instead of giving details about the archery contest, the author skims over that event to focus on the girls' reactions to their victory. Changing the pace enables the author to downplay the tournament win and focus on the girls' growing bond.

Reflect on Your Writing

Reread a narrative you wrote that has more than one paragraph. Have you varied the pace in the right places? Choose an important moment in your story. Think about ways to improve your pacing.

TRY SOME OF THESE IDEAS:

→ Find ways to skim over or briefly summarize routine events.

→ Expand important moments by adding interesting, believable dialogue between characters to make the scene seem realistic.

→ Build excitement and suspense by adding lively action and vivid descriptions.

After you revise your narrative, reread it. Have the changes to your pacing brought the events alive for your readers?

Wild Weather

by Laura Townsend

What's the weather like where you are? Sunny and warm? Snowy and cold? Is a storm predicted? Have you thought about the weather at all today?

Meteorologists, or scientists who study weather, always think about the weather. They also observe, measure, and record its changing patterns. Their goal is to better predict what the weather will be, especially when storms are about to strike.

What Causes Weather?

When predicting weather, scientists study air masses. An air mass is a large body of air with the same properties, such as temperature, air pressure, and water vapor.

A colder air mass doesn't mix well with a warmer air mass, and that can cause stormy weather! Cold air is heavier than warm air, so it pushes underneath a warm air mass. When warm air moves into a cold air mass, however, the opposite action occurs. Warm air is lighter, so it rises above the cold air.

Changes in the weather occur because air masses are always on the move. The area where two air masses meet is known as a *front.* When a warm air mass is moving into an area, it's called a warm front. When a cold air mass moves in, that area is called a cold front.

Scientists also study air pressure to predict the weather. Air pressure is the weight of air pressing down on you. High air pressure causes the weather to stay calm, but if air pressure begins to drop, watch out—this can lead to really wild weather!

Cold Front: Because cold air is heavier, a cold front pushes a warm air mass upward.

Warm Front: Warm air is lighter, so it lifts above a cold air mass.

KEY

■ warm air   ■ cold air

What Causes Hurricanes?

Hurricanes affect the weather in the United States each year. Beginning as tropical disturbances, some storms continue to gain force and size. Once their wind speeds reach 74 miles per hour, the huge, rotating storms are officially labeled hurricanes.

A hurricane forms over warm ocean waters. Its winds begin to circle around an area of low air pressure, creating clouds and thunderstorms. More warm, wet air gets pulled upward, causing the storm to become larger and stronger. Wind speeds build, air pressure drops, and the storm keeps strengthening because of the warm, wet air feeding it. Eventually, a dangerous hurricane is born.

Pushed ahead of a hurricane, the ocean's surface may rise by as much as 33 feet. These *storm surges* can be as wide as 100 miles and can smash into shorelines like bulldozers. If a hurricane comes ashore, it brings heavy rain, flooding, and damaging winds, causing great loss to people, animals, and property.

A hurricane may be as wide as 300 miles. It can travel thousands of miles and last for more than a week. Once it reaches cooler seas or moves across land, however, the hurricane loses its energy source. As a result, it begins to weaken.

A Look at a Hurricane

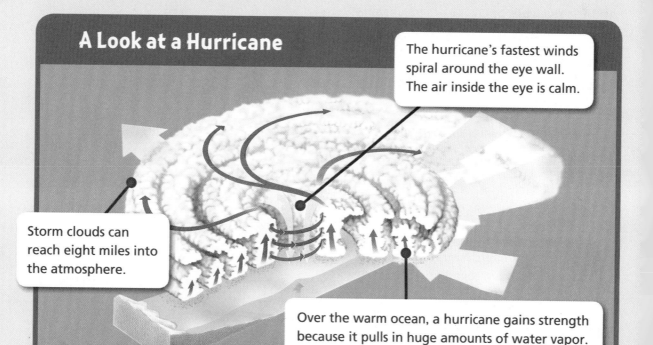

The hurricane's fastest winds spiral around the eye wall. The air inside the eye is calm.

Storm clouds can reach eight miles into the atmosphere.

Over the warm ocean, a hurricane gains strength because it pulls in huge amounts of water vapor.

What Causes Thunderstorms?

About 45,000 thunderstorms occur around the world every day, bringing rain, wind, lightning, thunder, and sometimes hail. These powerful storms develop when air masses of different temperatures come together.

Thunderstorms begin to form as warm, humid air rises rapidly. Then a cold front or strong winds push under the warmer air mass. As the rising air begins to cool, clouds take shape, heavy with water droplets and even ice crystals. Strong winds blow both upward and downward within the cloud. Finally, rain begins to fall, pulling cool air down with it. Strong electric charges build up at the bottom of the cloud, causing lightning and thunder.

While violent, these powerful storms are usually over within about an hour. Because the rain and cooler air prevent warm air from continuing to rise into the clouds, most thunderstorms will move away quickly.

When extremely strong thunderstorms occur, meteorologists become concerned about the possibility of another severe weather event—a tornado. Tornadoes form in less than one percent of all thunderstorms, but when they hit, they can destroy everything in their path.

Large amounts of warm air are pushed upward, forming a thundercloud. These upward movements of air, called updrafts, can reach speeds of 62 miles per hour.

What Causes Tornadoes?

A violent, twisting column of air racing across the plains may be exciting to see in a movie, but few people want to see one in real life. Some tornadoes generate the fastest winds on Earth. Their wind speeds may reach over 300 miles per hour.

Tornadoes form when winds spin a funnel, or column of air, at the base of a storm cloud. Rapidly rising air in the funnel pulls warm, humid air into it. The fast-spinning air creates an area of low air pressure in the funnel's center. Due to the low pressure, air on the ground continues to rush into the funnel and to join the cloud above. The swirling funnel begins to lengthen. If conditions are right, the funnel touches down, and the tornado begins to move along the ground.

These violent storms typically have narrow paths of destruction; nevertheless, their routes may cover many miles. Tornadoes are more difficult to predict than other storms. However, with advanced weather tracking, meteorologists are now better able to warn people and give them time to take cover.

cool air

spinning funnel cloud

warm air

Sudden changes in wind direction and speed create a violently spinning funnel that may become a dangerous tornado.

As meteorologists continue to learn about weather patterns, they will be able to more accurately predict the paths that storms may take. This means less chance for loss of life and property. With better forecasting, people have more time to prepare, so wild weather doesn't have to be so scary!

Tornadoes Strike
1974: A Super Outbreak
by Leonard Turner

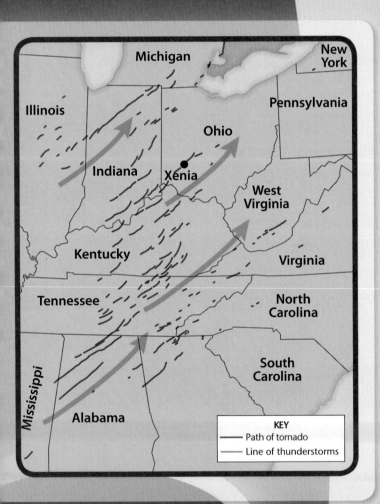

Map labels: Michigan, New York, Illinois, Pennsylvania, Ohio, Indiana, Xenia, West Virginia, Kentucky, Virginia, Tennessee, North Carolina, South Carolina, Mississippi, Alabama

KEY
— Path of tornado
— Line of thunderstorms

On April 3, 1974, a huge line of storms moved across several states, creating more than 100 tornadoes.

Few things in nature are more powerful than tornadoes. Their winds rage. They can strike quickly without warning and destroy everything in their path. In early April of 1974, a series of events occurred that illustrated their deadly power.

A huge stretch of the central United States—including parts of Texas, Iowa, Kansas, Nebraska, and as far east as Ohio—has been aptly nicknamed Tornado Alley due to the high frequency of tornadoes occurring there each year. On April 3 and 4, 1974, parts of this area as well as neighboring states experienced the greatest number of tornadoes in a single 24-hour period in history. One hundred and forty-eight tornadoes of all sizes struck with little warning.

Earlier in the week, meteorologists had reported that cold air was moving in over the central United States from Canada. At the same time, they noted that warm air was pushing north from the Gulf of Mexico. These air masses were sure to meet and cause major thunderstorms, but no one could accurately predict what would actually happen.

The outbreak began on the morning of April 2, when a huge line of thunderstorms moved across Tornado Alley. Soon, funnel clouds formed along a storm path that stretched for nearly 2,500 miles.

First Strikes

The first tornado to be reported hit Morris, Illinois, in the early afternoon. Small in size, the tornado did not cause any serious injuries. About an hour later, more tornadoes touched down in Tennessee and Georgia. Within ten minutes, still more tornadoes were spotted in several counties in Illinois and southern Indiana.

Then, around 3:30 in the afternoon, three separate storms moved over the small town of Xenia, Ohio. They joined together, creating one massive tornado. With winds of over 300 miles per hour, this deadly tornado touched down in a community that had little time to prepare.

For nine minutes, the enormous tornado roared through the town like a freight train. It ripped trees from the ground, tore down buildings, and tossed cars and trucks in the air as if they were toys. Luckily, most students had left school for the day, but seven schools, nine churches, and hundreds of homes were totally destroyed in this town of 27,000 people. By the time the tornado had left town, more than 30 people had been killed.

Kentucky was next to report tornadoes at 3:40 P.M. Central Time (CT), and within the hour, Alabama began reporting tornadoes.

Xenia, Ohio, was all but destroyed when a huge tornado touched down on April 3, 1974.

More Reports

The deadly outbreak wasn't over yet. Around 3:50 P.M. CT, Monticello, Indiana, was hit hard. Eight people were killed, over 350 were injured, and most of the downtown area was destroyed. The county's historic courthouse, built in 1894, was damaged so severely that it later had to be demolished.

Traveling at an average speed of 55 miles per hour, the tornado that ripped through Monticello also took out the Penn Central Railroad bridge. Several of the 250-pound railroad ties forming the bridge were lifted up and carried off by the powerful winds. Many were found over ten miles away, where they had been dropped like broken toothpicks.

The next day, tornadoes continued to develop and produce paths of destruction. Five more F5 tornadoes devastated the towns of Depauw, Indiana; Sayler Park, Ohio; Brandenburg, Kentucky; and Tanner and Guin, Alabama. Some 90 lives were lost as a result.

Finally, in the early evening of April 4, 1973, the last tornado hit Baton, North Carolina, causing more damage. In the end, 330 people lost their lives during this destructive tornado outbreak.

The tornadoes that struck the United States during the 1974 Super Tornado Outbreak differed greatly. Some lasted only minutes, and some were stronger than others. Twenty-three reached the F4 class, with wind speeds of up to 260 miles per hour. Six more reached the F5 class, with powerful winds greater than 260 miles per hour. Many more tornadoes formed but never touched the ground or caused any damage.

Most of the people who were affected had little warning of tornadoes that day. In 1974 scientists had limited technology for predicting or tracking tornadoes. Often, no one even knew that a tornado had formed until it was spotted.

Today, many more tools exist to help track severe weather. Meteorologists know where thunderstorms are forming and how severe they're likely to be. They can better identify the conditions in which tornadoes are likely to form so that warnings can be issued, giving people time to take cover.

Tornado prediction is still far from an exact science, but technological advances continue to be made. We will surely be better prepared when conditions are right for the next super tornado outbreak.

Classes of Tornadoes

Scale	Wind Speed (mph)
F0	40–72
F1	73–112
F2	113–157
F3	158–206
F4	207–260
F5	261–318

The Fujita scale gives scientists a way to classify tornadoes based on wind damage.

Cold, Hot, or What?

SCORCHING

HOT

COLD

FRIGID

Brrrrrr! When the temperature hits the bottom of a thermometer, it's *cold*. You might even say it's *frigid!* When the temperature hits the opposite end of the thermometer, it's extremely *hot*—maybe even *scorching!*

According to the meanings in a dictionary, *cold* and *frigid* are related—they're synonyms. However, the ideas suggested by the words differ. *Cold* and *frigid* bring to mind different connotations, or personal feelings and reactions.

Some words suggest more positive feelings, while others suggest negative ones. *Scorching* and *frigid* create strong— even extreme—reactions, while *warm* and *cool* create milder feelings. Connotations often differ in degree, just like temperatures.

1 With a partner, discuss the connotations that these words bring to mind: *tepid, sweltering, frosty,* and *chilly*. Then, based on their "degree" of connotation, decide where you might place each word between *scorching* and *frigid* on a thermometer like the one on the left.

2 Draw another thermometer and write *weak* at one end and *powerful* at the other. Based on word connotations, decide where on the thermometer to place the words shown below. How many other related words can you add?

**forceful   wimpy   mighty
frail   strong**

As Dark as MIDNIGHT!

In "Wild Weather" and "Tornadoes Strike," the authors use similes, metaphors, and other figurative language in their descriptions. A simile compares two things that are unlike by using the word *like* or *as*. A metaphor compares two different things by saying that one thing *is* another.

> For nine minutes, the enormous <u>tornado roared</u> through the town <u>like a freight train</u>.

In the simile above, the sound of the tornado is said to be similar to the roar of a freight train. By pointing out a way the two are alike, you can imagine how terrifying a tornado must be!

> The twisting <u>tornado is a vacuum cleaner</u>, sucking up everything in its path.

In this metaphor, the destruction of a tornado is compared to the action of a vacuum cleaner. Can you picture the destruction it causes?

For each sentence, identify the things being compared. Then write to explain how the things are alike.

1. Like bulldozers, storm surges smash into shorelines and cause great loss to people, animals, and property.

2. The tropical storm was a sponge, soaking up the warm, humid air.

3. Lightning exploded like brilliant fireworks between the storm clouds.

4. The hikers baked in the furnace created by the desert sun.

Linked!

When you write to inform or explain, it's important to use links to connect your ideas together.

To do this, use . . .

- **headings** to show how parts in a longer piece are organized. Headings also let readers know when you're shifting to a new idea.

- **transition words and phrases,** such as *in contrast, however, in addition,* and *finally* to link one idea to another or to show sequence.

- **a conclusion** to wrap up your ideas. A good conclusion links to the opening of the report. It restates the main points and makes a final comment.

How did the author link ideas between the introduction and the conclusion in "Tornadoes Strike"? What final comment did he make?

Introduction

Few things in nature are more powerful than tornadoes. Their winds rage. They can strike quickly without warning and destroy everything in their path. In early April of 1974, a series of events occurred that illustrated their deadly power.

Conclusion

Tornado prediction is still far from an exact science, but technological advances continue to be made. We will surely be better prepared when conditions are right for the next super tornado outbreak.

Reflect on Your Writing

Reread a report you have written, or use another longer piece of informational writing. Have you linked your ideas? What improvements can you make? Ask yourself questions.

Have I . . .

▶ used headings, if needed, to show the way the parts are organized?

▶ supplied transitional words and phrases to link ideas?

▶ included a strong conclusion that links to my introduction?

Find ways to revise your report to include these key links. Your revised writing should help your readers link to your ideas.

JOURNEY TO DISCOVERY

In the next section of this magazine you will read about animals from the distant past and from right now, including a fish that lives in both times! You'll explore a cave of crystals, a palace in a cliff, and a prehistoric tar pit (don't get too close).

You'll read poems and stories about fossils and mysterious deer, and travel even farther in a lot of fun activities.

Your journey to discovery begins when you turn the page!

JOURNEY TO DISCOVERY

Skywoman's Rescue

The Haudenosaunee myth "Skywoman and Turtle" is in Lesson 6 of the *Journeys* Student Book, page 164. Read this play version of the myth. Then tell how the two versions are alike and different.

> **Setting:**
> *The dark, watery world below the sky*
>
> **Characters**
> *Narrator • Turtle • Toad • Otter*
> *Goose 1 • Goose 2 • Skywoman*

Narrator: The animals living below the sky led a peaceful life.

Toad: *(Lazily)* Should I swim, or should I take a nap? I'll nap.

Narrator: But one day two Geese flew down with news.

Goose 1: *(Landing in the water)* Guess what! Skywoman dreamed about a hole in the clouds! And her dream inspired the Chief to uproot the Great Tree!

Toad: Too bad. I liked that tree.

Goose 2: Now there really is a hole in the clouds!

Otter: *(Peering upward)* And Skywoman must have fallen through, because here she comes!

Turtle: Geese! Can you fly up and catch her?

Geese: We can—and we will! *(They fly off.)*

Narrator: While the Geese took off into the sky, Turtle thought about what to do next.

Turtle: Skywoman will need someplace to land. I doubt if she can swim.

Narrator: Turtle tilted her head, pondering. Finally she came to a decision.

Turtle: Toad! Swim down and bring up lots of mud!

Toad: Mud? That's your plan?

Turtle: As much mud as you can carry! Hurry!

Narrator: Toad dove into the water. Meanwhile, the Geese circled lower and lower with Skywoman between their wings. At last, Toad came to the surface. His mouth bulged with mud.

Turtle: Good! Now, you and Otter spread the mud over my shell, good and thick!

Otter: *(Spreading mud)* This will make a nice soft landing.

Narrator: Just in time, the Geese came down on Turtle's back with Skywoman.

Skywoman: Thank you, noble animals. You rescued me!

Toad: No problem. Hey, you have seeds!

Skywoman: Yes, I grabbed them from the Great Tree as I fell. *(She scatters the seeds on the mud.)*

Narrator: The seeds took root. Soon the mud became the earth, thick with plants and full of new life. And later, Skywoman gave birth to twins. They became the first people.

Toad: All because of me! *(Toad exits with a splash.)*

ANiMaLS ON

Leaving Home

On a warm summer day, a tiny striped fish wiggles out of the gravel of a riverbed in Northern California. For the next few months this young Pacific salmon, called a fry, explores the section of the river where she was born, feeding on insects and plants. Then instinct, knowledge she was born with, tells her to swim downstream. Tumbling over rocks and through rapids, the salmon finally reaches the mouth of the river, where it meets the sea. Saltwater and freshwater mix and the salmon spends a few weeks feeding on small shellfish as she doubles in size, loses her stripes, and turns a shining silver.

Then the young salmon travels out to sea, swimming for thousands of miles into the ocean. In a few years she will find her way back across the ocean and up the river to the exact section where she was born. How can she do this?

Animals have five senses, just as people do: sight, hearing, touch, taste, and smell. To navigate, they use these senses and other abilities that people don't have, such as echolocation, in ways that scientists are still trying to understand.

These sockeye salmon are returning to their home to spawn, or lay eggs.

Bird Maps and Compasses

It is easy to get to places you've been to many times before. But traveling a long distance or an unknown route takes more planning. A map and a compass are often helpful for such trips. The map shows you how to get from one place to another. The compass can tell you in what direction you are moving.

Every year hundreds of species of birds take long trips, too. They fly hundreds and thousands of miles from one home to another. In the fall, they fly to warmer climates where food is plentiful all winter. When spring comes, they fly back to raise their young where they were born. For a long time people wondered where the birds went and what routes they took.

A crane in flight.

Why Bees Sing and Dance

Honeybees work together in a hive. Young bees work inside the hive. Older bees go outside to gather pollen and nectar from flowers to make honey. At first they make dozens of short flights to learn the lay of the land. Next, they learn the direction the sun appears to move. Finally, they fly as far as three miles from their hive to gather pollen.

Bees use their sense of smell as well as eyesight to find flowers. They use the sun to find their way home. On cloudy days, they look for landmarks they have learned. Back at the hive, they offer nectar they found to the other bees. Then the bees dance. Sometimes they move in circles. At other times, they zigzag or "waggle."

Beekeepers have long known that bees dance, but it was not until 1947 that scientists discovered why. When honeybees dance, they are telling the other bees where to find food. Researchers also discovered that the sounds bees make while dancing give information about finding flowers. The bees need the whole song and dance routine to learn how to return to the flowers and get nectar, too.

A honeybee's circular dance means flowers are nearby. A waggle dance signals that the flowers are farther away.

Why Bats Squeak

Bats also make sounds that humans cannot hear. But these sounds are not rumbles. They are high-pitched squeaks. Bats use these squeaks and their excellent hearing to find their way in the dark. They do so through *echolocation*, using echoes to locate something.

If you make a loud sound in a large, empty room, you will hear that sound come back to you as an echo. Echoes are created when sound waves move through the air, hit something, and bounce back. All sounds move in this way, bouncing back if they hit a solid object. But human hearing is not good enough to hear most echoes.

Bats, however, do hear these echoes. Bats make their squeaking sounds as they fly through the dark in search of food. The squeaks bounce off trees, houses, and other objects. This is useful in finding prey because echoes even bounce off insects! Amazingly, these bouncing echoes tell bats how far away the insect is, which direction it is moving, and how fast it is flying. Bats can even tell how fat and juicy the insect is! Echolocation is important to bats, because insects are their main source of food.

Sound waves from a bat's squeak bounce off an insect and travel back to the bat as an echo. In this way bats can find their dinner.

The Move

Elephant Talk

Elephants trumpet when they are excited or alarmed. Mother elephants hum to their newborn babies. But people who study elephants have noticed something odd. A herd might be grazing peacefully in the African grasslands. Suddenly they all lift their heads, flap their ears, and begin to walk together in the same direction. They may walk for miles and then meet another herd. The elephants greet each other with loud trumpeting calls, flapping their ears and twisting their trunks together. It's a gigantic family reunion.

How did they find each other?

The elephants didn't see each other. If the wind was not blowing the right way, their sense of smell didn't help them. Scientists were puzzled. Dr. Katy Payne solved the puzzle when she recorded elephant sounds at a slow speed. She listened to the tapes at normal speed and heard elephant sounds no human had ever heard before. They were deep rumbles, too low for our ears to hear. But elephants could hear them from miles away. Scientists call this *infrasound*.

Sound moves in waves through the air. Low sounds like the elephants' rumbles move in long waves that can travel many miles. So elephants rumble back and forth to find each other.

Elephants travel together in groups across the African plains. They follow infrasonic calls their relatives make, sounds too low for human ears.

Leaving Home

On a warm summer day, a tiny striped fish wiggles out of the gravel of a riverbed in Northern California. For the next few months this young Pacific salmon, called a fry, explores the section of the river where she was born, feeding on insects and plants. Then instinct, knowledge she was born with, tells her to swim downstream. Tumbling over rocks and through rapids, the salmon finally reaches the mouth of the river, where it meets the sea. Saltwater and freshwater mix and the salmon spends a few weeks feeding on small shellfish as she doubles in size, loses her stripes, and turns a shining silver.

Then the young salmon travels out to sea, swimming for thousands of miles into the ocean. In a few years she will find her way back across the ocean and up the river to the exact section where she was born. How can she do this?

Animals have five senses, just as people do: sight, hearing, touch, taste, and smell. To navigate, they use these senses and other abilities that people don't have, such as echolocation, in ways that scientists are still trying to understand.

These sockeye salmon are returning to their home to spawn, or lay eggs.

Geese: We can—and we will! *(They fly off.)*

Narrator: While the Geese took off into the sky, Turtle thought about what to do next.

Turtle: Skywoman will need someplace to land. I doubt if she can swim.

Narrator: Turtle tilted her head, pondering. Finally she came to a decision.

Turtle: Toad! Swim down and bring up lots of mud!

Toad: Mud? That's your plan?

Turtle: As much mud as you can carry! Hurry!

Narrator: Toad dove into the water. Meanwhile, the Geese circled lower and lower with Skywoman between their wings. At last, Toad came to the surface. His mouth bulged with mud.

Turtle: Good! Now, you and Otter spread the mud over my shell, good and thick!

Otter: *(Spreading mud)* This will make a nice soft landing.

Narrator: Just in time, the Geese came down on Turtle's back with Skywoman.

Skywoman: Thank you, noble animals. You rescued me!

Toad: No problem. Hey, you have seeds!

Skywoman: Yes, I grabbed them from the Great Tree as I fell. *(She scatters the seeds on the mud.)*

Narrator: The seeds took root. Soon the mud became the earth, thick with plants and full of new life. And later, Skywoman gave birth to twins. They became the first people.

Toad: All because of me! *(Toad exits with a splash.)*

Skywoman's Rescue

The Haudenosaunee myth "Skywoman and Turtle" is in Lesson 6 of the *Journeys* Student Book, page 164. Read this play version of the myth. Then tell how the two versions are alike and different.

> **Setting:**
> *The dark, watery world below the sky*
>
> **Characters**
> Narrator • Turtle • Toad • Otter
> Goose 1 • Goose 2 • Skywoman

Narrator: The animals living below the sky led a peaceful life.

Toad: (*Lazily*) Should I swim, or should I take a nap? I'll nap.

Narrator: But one day two Geese flew down with news.

Goose 1: (*Landing in the water*) Guess what! Skywoman dreamed about a hole in the clouds! And her dream inspired the Chief to uproot the Great Tree!

Toad: Too bad. I liked that tree.

Goose 2: Now there really is a hole in the clouds!

Otter: (*Peering upward*) And Skywoman must have fallen through, because here she comes!

Turtle: Geese! Can you fly up and catch her?

3

JOURNEY TO DISCOVERY

Lesson 26

1

JOURNEY TO DISCOVERY

In the next section of this magazine you will read about animals from the distant past and from right now, including a fish that lives in both times! You'll explore a cave of crystals, a palace in a cliff, and a prehistoric tar pit (don't get too close).

You'll read poems and stories about fossils and mysterious deer, and travel even farther in a lot of fun activities.

Your journey to discovery begins when you turn the page!

Reflect on Your Writing

Reread a report you have written, or use another longer piece of informational writing. Have you linked your ideas? What improvements can you make? Ask yourself questions.

Have I . . .

▶ used headings, if needed, to show the way the parts are organized?

▶ supplied transitional words and phrases to link ideas?

▶ included a strong conclusion that links to my introduction?

Find ways to revise your report to include these key links. Your revised writing should help your readers link to your ideas.

Linked!

When you write to inform or explain, it's important to use links to connect your ideas together.

To do this, use . . .

- **headings** to show how parts in a longer piece are organized. Headings also let readers know when you're shifting to a new idea.

- **transition words and phrases,** such as *in contrast, however, in addition,* **and** *finally* to link one idea to another or to show sequence.

- **a conclusion** to wrap up your ideas. A good conclusion links to the opening of the report. It restates the main points and makes a final comment.

How did the author link ideas between the introduction and the conclusion in "Tornadoes Strike"? What final comment did he make?

Introduction

Few things in nature are more powerful than tornadoes. Their winds rage. They can strike quickly without warning and destroy everything in their path. In early April of 1974, a series of events occurred that illustrated their deadly power.

Conclusion

Tornado prediction is still far from an exact science, but technological advances continue to be made. We will surely be better prepared when conditions are right for the next super tornado outbreak.

As Dark as MIDNIGHT!

In "Wild Weather" and "Tornadoes Strike," the authors use similes, metaphors, and other figurative language in their descriptions. A simile compares two things that are unlike by using the word *like* or *as*. A metaphor compares two different things by saying that one thing *is* another.

> For nine minutes, the enormous <u>tornado roared</u> through the town <u>like a freight train</u>.

In the simile above, the sound of the tornado is said to be similar to the roar of a freight train. By pointing out a way the two are alike, you can imagine how terrifying a tornado must be!

> The twisting <u>tornado is a vacuum cleaner</u>, sucking up everything in its path.

In this metaphor, the destruction of a tornado is compared to the action of a vacuum cleaner. Can you picture the destruction it causes?

For each sentence, identify the things being compared. Then write to explain how the things are alike.

1. Like bulldozers, storm surges smash into shorelines and cause great loss to people, animals, and property.

2. The tropical storm was a sponge, soaking up the warm, humid air.

3. Lightning exploded like brilliant fireworks between the storm clouds.

4. The hikers baked in the furnace created by the desert sun.

Researchers now know that migrating birds, such as cranes, are guided by their own sorts of maps and compasses. But it has taken many decades to uncover the secrets of these navigation tools. In the 1800s, scientists started putting bands around birds' legs. The bands contained a name and address. When people found the banded birds, they contacted the person named on the band and told that tracker where and when they had found the bird. In this simple way, scientists learned a lot about where birds traveled, where they stopped, and how fast they moved.

Today scientists still put light aluminum bands on birds' legs. They also use new ways of tracking birds—airplanes, computers, tiny radio transmitters, and satellites. Scientists have answered many questions about how birds navigate.

Endangered whooping cranes learn a migration route by following an ultralight aircraft.

Some birds migrate in a flock. You may have seen Canada geese flying high in the sky in the form of a V. Young birds follow their parents and learn the route that the older geese have traveled before. They may follow a river and remember what it looks like. Certain sounds or smells will stay in their memory. Also, like captains on sailing ships long ago, birds use the position of the sun and stars as a compass to find their way.

Birds and many other animals also use earth's magnetic field to navigate. Chemicals in these animals' brains allow them to sense the magnetic field and travel in the right direction. But scientists are still researching how this happens. They think some birds may actually be able to see earth's magnetic field.

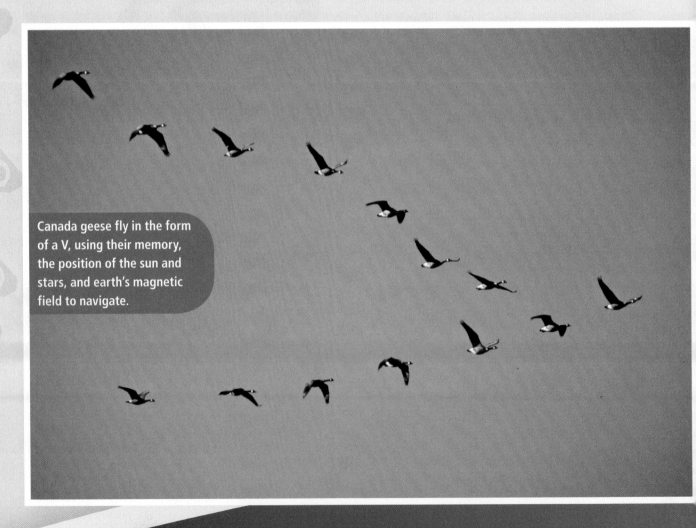

Canada geese fly in the form of a V, using their memory, the position of the sun and stars, and earth's magnetic field to navigate.

Returning Home

After leaving the river, the Pacific salmon lives in the ocean for the next few years. Eventually, though, she begins her return journey. She is going home to the stream where she was born to lay eggs, or spawn. How does a salmon remember the route she took years before and find her way back?

Scientists don't know all the answers, but here's what they think is happening: a Pacific salmon feels the temperature of the water and the ocean currents. She tastes how the saltiness of the water changes in different places. She sees the location of the sun and the star patterns at night. Like a migrating bird, she can sense the earth's magnetic field to find her way.

Finally, the salmon remembers the smell of her birthplace. The plants that grow and the leaves that fall from the trees create a special odor for each stream.

She swims up over the rocks and rapids on her last journey. She will lay eggs to create the next generation of Pacific salmon. Then she will die, leaving her fry to make their own journeys using instinct and navigation skills they inherit from their parents.

Each year, thousands of salmon return to the waters where they hatched. They use many clues to find their way back.

The Whale

by Douglas Florian

Big as a street —

With fins, not feet —

I'm full of blubber,

With skin like rubber.

When I breathe out,

I spew a spout.

I swim by the shore

And eat more and more.

I'm very, very hard to ignore.

Wild Geese

by Sandra Olson Liatsos

When I watch
Their flock in flight
And when I hear their cries
I wonder how
They always know
Their way through
Distant skies.

ANIMAL MATCH

In the article "Animals on the Move," you read about the abilities and habits of many different animals. In the left column below is a list of animals mentioned in the article. The column on the right lists different animal characteristics. On a separate piece of paper, match each description to the animal it describes best. Review the article if you're not sure!

1. Salmon   A. makes a rumbling sound that people cannot hear

2. Elephant   B. moves in a zigzag motion
3. Bat   C. returns to its place of birth to spawn
4. Honeybee   D. uses high-pitched squeaks to find its way

WILD SIMILES

Similes are comparisons that use the word *like* or *as.* A simile helps people understand something by comparing it to something else. In the poem "The Whale," for example, the whale says that it is as "Big as a street... With skin like rubber."

Create two or three similes about an animal mentioned in "Animals on the Move" or about an animal of your choice. Use features from the chart below. Take turns reading your similes with a partner.

Feature	Example
size	as tall as a tree
texture	as smooth as glass
movement	racing like the wind
color	as black as ink
sound	cooing like a flute

Wild

In "Animals on the Move" you read about how salmon, bats, bees, birds, and elephants travel. You read how they use their five senses. You also learned about special abilities they have, such as echolocation, the waggle dance, and steering by earth's magnetic field.

Choose an animal from the article or another animal you know about. Write a story about an adventure it has while traveling.

Traveler

Use a story map to plan the setting and the plot, including a problem and solution. Does the animal get lost? Is it trying to get home? Does it escape from danger?

As you write, include dialogue. Maybe human characters in your story talk about the animal. Maybe one animal speaks to another. Dialogue is a good way of developing the plot of a story.

There have been many books written about animals that go on journeys. *Lassie Come-Home*, by Eric Knight, is about a collie that makes a long and difficult journey home after being separated from its master. *The Black Stallion*, by Walter Farley, tells the tale of a beautiful black horse that is shipwrecked on a desert island with a boy until both are rescued.

Another well-read animal adventure is *The Incredible Journey* by Sheila Burnford. A Labrador retriever, a bull terrier, and a Siamese cat face many obstacles on a journey of two hundred miles before returning home.

Your story may become the next classic!

Mysteries at Cliff Palace

Cast of Characters
Narrator
Ruben
Rosa
Mom
Dad
Ranger Jenkins

Narrator: Ten-year-old Ruben, his older sister Rosa, and their parents are visiting Mesa Verde National Park in Colorado. They're with a group waiting for a ranger-guided tour of the cliff dwellings.

Ruben: Wow, this is going to be great! I'm going to solve one of the great mysteries of ancient North America, with the help of my trusty notebook!

Mom: Just look how many dwellings are built into the cliff alcove down there!

Ruben: All those walls and towers inside the ledge are really cool!

Mom: This was all built by the Ancestral Puebloan people.

Dad: That's right. These dwellings have been here about 800 years.

Ruben: I can't wait to see Cliff Palace up close. I'm sure I can find some clues to the mystery of why the people all disappeared.

Rosa: Right, Ruben. You can't even keep track of your lucky pen. So how can you solve a real mystery?

Ruben: Don't remind me, Rosa. I looked all over the car for it.

Dad: Hey, Ruben, here comes the ranger.

Mom: I bet she knows a lot about the Puebloan mystery.

Narrator: Ranger Jenkins arrives and introduces herself.

Ranger Jenkins: Gather round, everyone. We'll be descending 100 feet into the canyon. It's quite a trek, so be prepared.

Ruben: Aren't there five eight-foot ladders to climb?

Ranger Jenkins: It's challenging, but you can do it.

Rosa (to Ruben): I hope I can. It's so hot!

Ruben: I'll push you along if you need it. Just promise you'll tell me if you find any clues to the mystery.

Dad: Rosa, didn't you have a question for Ranger Jenkins?

Rosa: Yes! Why is this park named Mesa Verde? Doesn't that mean "green table" in Spanish?

Ranger Jenkins: Exactly! You see these huge, flat hills all around us? They're sometimes called plateaus. But they're as flat as tabletops, so they're also called mesas. And *verde* just refers to all the green plants and trees growing here.

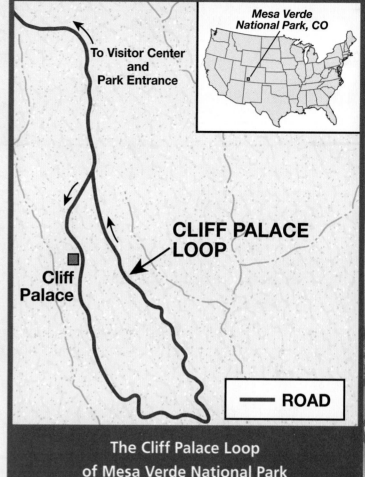

The Cliff Palace Loop
of Mesa Verde National Park

Narrator: Ruben waves his hand urgently.

Ruben: I've been reading a lot about the Ancestral Puebloans who built these cities like Cliff Palace. I read that at some time they just left here, and I'm trying to figure out why.

Ranger Jenkins: Great question, Ruben. Historians have been puzzling over this mystery for a long time. I'd like to hear your ideas.

Ruben: Well... I'm not sure, but—

Rosa: What *I* want to know is how they built those dwellings.

Ranger Jenkins: We'll talk a bit about that during the tour, Rosa. Okay, did everyone see the alcoves in the canyon walls? These cliffs are made of sandstone and shale, and sandstone is soft—it easily breaks and crumbles away. Over time, that breaking and crumbling carved the alcoves out of the rock.

Dad: So when did the Ancestral Puebloans start living here?

Ranger Jenkins: They came to this area around 600 C.E., but it wasn't until around 1200 that they built these dwellings in the cliffs. Let's go take a closer look at their handiwork. Watch where you're walking, everyone. The steps down are really rough and uneven.

Narrator: Ruben doesn't notice he's dropped his notebook on the steps. His mother hands it to him, and then goes on ahead to take pictures.

Dad: How about that pen you were missing, Ruben? Did you find it yet?

Ruben: I don't know where it went, Dad! It's not in any of my pockets.

Rosa: See, I told you. How can he solve an ancient mystery? He can't even solve the mystery of his missing stuff!

Ruben: Dad, tell Rosa to stop teasing! In fact—I bet she has my pen.

Rosa: I do not!

Dad: What does it look like?

Ruben: It has a digital thermometer on it, so I can tell the temperature! I always use it when I take tests.

Ranger Jenkins: Listen up, everyone. This round pit in front of us is called a kiva. A kiva is a ceremonial room. The Ancestral Puebloans built kivas for special religious ceremonies. If you look over there, you can see where the people climbed up the cliffs to the top of the mesa farm. And of course, this is Cliff Palace. Cliff Palace has twenty-three kivas and 150 rooms, which housed about 100 people, we think.

Ruben: Man, look at all these cliff dwellings!

Dad: And those towers. Just think of the work that went into building all this!

Ruben: Yeah, but the people only lived here for around 75 to 100 years. Why would they just leave?

Rosa: Maybe they were thirsty, like me. It is so hot here! And I already drank all my water.

Ruben: Hey, you could be right, Rosa! There was a drought here, sometime, wasn't there?

Ranger Jenkins: Yes, there was! The drought began in 1276 and may have lasted for twenty years. A lot of people think that Ancestral Puebloans left after their crops died and they didn't have enough food.

On the other hand, the people had survived droughts in the past. They stored food to prepare for hard times. Why would this drought drive them away if they had survived others?

Ruben: Don't some people think maybe a war forced them to leave?

Ranger Jenkins: Right, there may have been a war. It might have started with one group raiding another for food.

Ruben: Or maybe the different groups fought for each other's land, to get the best places to grow crops and find water.

Narrator: After discussing their ideas with Ranger Jenkins, Ruben decides to look for clues.

Mom: Ruben, did you see where Rosa went?

Ruben: Mom! All these dwellings are made of sandstone bricks. The Puebloans made them one by one—by hand! So why leave after all that work?

Dad: It's great that you're keeping notes on this mystery, Ruben. But you didn't see Rosa wander off?

Ruben: Wait—my notebook! Dad, I lost it again!

Mom: We'll look for your notebook, Ruben, once we find Rosa.

Dad: I'll go see if she's with that group over there.

Ranger Jenkins: It's almost time to go. Take a few more minutes to look around, and then we'll climb those ladders up the cliff.

Mom: Quick, let's check all around the dwellings.

Narrator: Ruben looks around. He finds Rosa sitting in the shade of a rock wall near one of the Cliff Palace dwellings.

Ruben: What are you doing way over here, Rosa?

Rosa: Looking for shade! I was really hot and tired. I just needed to get out of the sun.

Ruben: You should have told Mom where you were going.

Rosa: I know. I was just going to sit here for a minute. But then I started looking at these cool bricks. And I started thinking how terrible it must have been to have no water here!

Ruben: That *could* be why the Ancestral Puebloans left, even though they worked so hard to build this city.

Rosa: So you haven't found out the reason for sure? Now I'm really wondering about it, too.

Ruben: No. And my notebook's lost again.

Rosa: Here it is. You left it by a tower, so I picked it up for you.

Ruben: Great! Do you have my pen, too?

Rosa: I promise I do not have your pen, Ruben. I wish I did. Then I could see exactly how hot it is out here! But being here makes me want to help solve this mystery.

Ruben: Good. But we'd better get back. It's almost time to go.

Narrator: Rosa and Ruben return to the group. Their parents are happy to see Rosa safe. The tour is about to end.

Ranger Jenkins: So, Ruben. Before we go, have you solved the mystery of the Ancestral Puebloans?

Ruben: Nope. But at least I have a few theories.

Mom: Okay, I'm ready to climb this ladder.

Ruben: Wait! Hold on, Mom! What's that sticking out of your back pocket?

Rosa: Oh, my gosh!

Ruben: Looks like a digital thermometer. It's my lucky pen!

Mom: Goodness, this thing? I found it on the ground near our car after we got here. I had no idea it was yours, Ruben. Here you go!

Dad: Well, we solved the mysteries of the lost Rosa, the lost notebook, and the lost pen today. Not bad for one day's work.

Ruben: Yeah, and now that I have my lucky pen back, I might solve the Ancestral Puebloans mystery in a few years!

Ranger Jenkins: With some good research, you just might! Now, everybody—up we go!

CAVE OF THE CRYSTALS

Imagine yourself one thousand feet underground, drilling a new tunnel in an old zinc and lead mine. Suddenly your drill bursts through the rock wall. What you see takes your breath away. Huge crystals fill a cave from end to end, floor to ceiling. They shimmer like moonlight. But before you can explore the cave, you are hit with air as hot as a blast from a furnace.

Two mineworkers, Juan and Pedro Sanchez, discovered this amazing "Cave of the Crystals" in 2000 at the Naica Mine in the state of Chihuahua, Mexico. They didn't stay long, for the intense heat drove them away.

The mine owners put an iron door at the mouth of the cave. Scientists came to study the cave, but because of the heat, they could stay inside for only a few minutes at a time.

The Cave of the Crystals is located in the desert of northern Mexico.

Inside Mexico's Cave of the Crystals

Scientists found the crystals were made of selenite gypsum, a translucent, light-colored mineral. The cave had just the right combination of minerals, water, and temperature to grow the crystals. The cave had once been filled with water, and heat from the earth's core kept the water at about 136 degrees Fahrenheit. This heated water caused some of the crystals to grow 36 feet long, about as tall as a three-story house! These are some of the largest natural crystals ever found.

Another team of scientists is now exploring the whole cave, which is nearly as large as a basketball court. They had to invent special clothing and breathing equipment for their work. Now they can stay inside for up to an hour at a time.

Water pumps keep the Naica Mine from filling with water. But without water the crystals will not grow any larger. Should the owners stop pumping out the water, so that the caves will flood again and the crystals will grow even larger? Or should they keep on pumping out the water, so that people can visit the cave? What would you do?

It took hundreds of thousands of years for the 36-foot crystals to get that big.

Places and Names: A Traveler's Guide

By J. Patrick Lewis

So many places have fabulous names,
Like Fried, North Dakota,
The Court of St. James,
Siberia, Nigeria, Elyria, Peru,
The White Nile, Black Sea,
And Kalamazoo!
The Great Wall of China, South Pole and Loch Ness,
And 104 Fairview—that's my address!

Thousands of spaces are places to be—
Discover the World of GE-OG-RA-PHY!

Travel by boat or by car or by plane
To visit East Africa, Singapore, Spain.
Go by yourself or invite a good friend,
But traveling by poem is what I recommend.

Los libros

By Francisco X. Alarcón

pasaportes
de talla mayor

que nos permiten
viajar

a dondequiera
cuandoquiera

y no dejar
de soñar

Books

oversized
passports

that let us
travel

anywhere
anytime

and keep on
dreaming

Think about Ruben, Rosa, and Ranger Jenkins in "Mysteries at Cliff Palace." Each one shows special personality traits. Read the traits below. Then match each one to the character who best shows that trait.

a knowledgeable

b curious

c teasing

d forgetful

e helpful

How does each trait contribute to the character's role in the story?

On a sheet of paper, draw a comic strip. Show characters' traits through their words.

Sensing the Cave

Imagine a hike to the Cave of the Crystals or another kind of cave. Think about the details your five senses would give you. On a separate sheet of paper, make a word web like the one on this page. Fill in each oval with sensory details for that sense. Below are two examples.

Use your web to write a description of your hike. A description can include an idiom, a phrase whose meaning is different from the meanings of its words. Think about the idiom "takes your breath away" in the first paragraph of "Cave of the Crystals." Discuss with a partner what that phrase means.

Smell

Sight

Taste
salty trail mix

Cave

Hearing

Touch
wet rocks

Bon Voyage!

Egypt

Hawaii

Hawaii? Egypt? The South Pole? Travel brochures are a great way to learn about places you've never visited. They give you a lot of details so you can imagine what a visit there would be like. Would you like to go to Mesa Verde National Park? Are you ready to explore the Cave of the Crystals? Or is there some other place you've visited that you really enjoyed?

Create a travel brochure about one of these places. Use details from "Mysteries at Cliff Palace" or "Cave of the Crystals" if you choose to write about either of these. If you write about someplace else, try to remember the most interesting details about that place.

South Pole

To start, fold a piece of letter-sized paper in half or in thirds. This will give your brochure a cover and some places inside for information. Title your brochure and make the cover colorful and interesting. Inside, give your readers details that would make them want to visit. Remember to write in a way that uses all the senses. If you paint a picture with words, your readers will easily imagine the place—and they'll want to visit it themselves!

To help you as you write, think about these questions:

What is unique about the destination?

What is the weather like?

What kinds of activities are offered?

Will visitors need special clothing?

Where can visitors stay?

Finally, draw pictures or cut out photos from magazines to illustrate your brochure. Bon voyage!

FOSSILS

A PEEK INTO THE PAST

Big news came out of Fairbanks, Alaska, in the fall of 2007. A ten-year-old boy named Jared Post had made a fantastic find. While walking home from school, Jared noticed a big, jagged rock half buried in the ground. Instantly curious, he dug the rock out. He noticed that it had what he called "weird engravings" on its underside. Jared felt pretty sure he had found something special—a fossil.

The young student's hunch was right. After bringing the toaster-sized object home, Jared and his dad searched the Internet for information. They discovered that the strange "rock" was in fact the tooth of a woolly mammoth, a giant mammal that lived during the Ice Age. The Ice Age occurred between 1.6 million and 10,000 years ago. In other words, that tooth was old!

The huge mammoth tooth Jared Post found weighed seven pounds. Jared is deciding whether to keep the tooth or donate it to a museum.

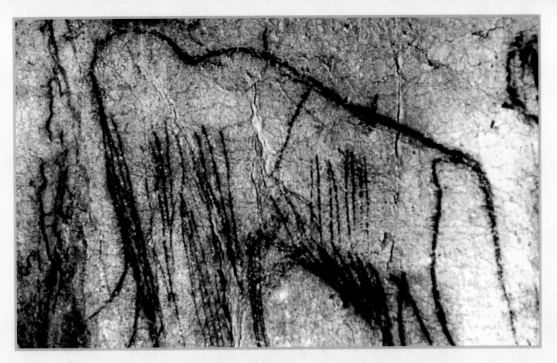

This drawing of a woolly mammoth was found on a cave wall in France.

Traces of the Past

Today, mammoths are extinct, meaning they no longer exist. Scientists can learn about them only by studying whatever remains they can find, such as bones, tusks, and teeth.

Animal teeth give a lot of information. By studying teeth, scientists can make a good guess about an animal's diet. Carnivores, or meat-eating animals, have sharp canine teeth to stab and hold on to prey. Herbivores are plant eaters, so they have large molars for chewing plants.

Although mammoths roamed throughout much of North America, Europe, Asia, and Africa, their bones and teeth are found mainly in areas with very cold weather. Any ideas why? It's because bones and teeth buried in frozen ground are less likely to be damaged. It's not surprising that Jared's mammoth tooth lasted 10,000 years or more. In his hometown of Fairbanks, the temperature stays below freezing more than half the year!

The pointed teeth of carnivores are much different than herbivore teeth.

Imagine a Woolly Mammoth!

For about two million years, woolly mammoths roamed the northern plains of Europe, North America, and Asia. Then, about 10,000 years ago, they disappeared, leaving only fossilized clues to their presence.

Thought to be early ancestors of today's elephants, these giant beasts were covered in dense shaggy hair. A thick layer of fat protected them from the cold. Teeth such as the one Jared discovered, probably a molar, indicates they were grass and leaf eaters. They used their long curving tusks, scientists believe, to shovel snow off the ground to reach buried plants.

Mammoths weighed about six to eight tons and stood about nine feet tall. Imagine an animal standing about as high as a one-story house and weighing as much as three or four full-sized pickup trucks.

"Just thinking about mammoths walking around my neighborhood 10,000 years ago is amazing!" Jared Post told reporters.

● **Mammoth fossil sites**

Dots on this map show some of the major North American sites where mammoth fossils have been found.

Fossils have given us most of the clues about the woolly mammoth.

One Girl's Remarkable Finds

Another super-successful young fossil hunter was Mary Anning, who was born on the south coast of England. Mary got quite a head start on recent fossil finders. She discovered the skeleton of a giant sea creature when she was about eleven years old. That was in 1810!

Scientists had never seen anything like the bones Mary found. They named it *ichthyosaurus* (ick thee oh SOR us), from the Greek words for fish and lizard. But it was not a fish at all. Later research proved it to be the fossilized body of a giant sea reptile.

Mary got credit for finding the very first ichthyosaur fossil. But she discovered others as well. In 1821, she found two—one five feet long and the other almost twenty feet long. These discoveries started a fossil craze in England.

Three-year-old Kaleb Kidd in La Crosse, Wisconsin, holds the woolly mammoth tooth he found.

A Very Good Year

Jared wasn't the only young discoverer to come across a mammoth's tooth in 2007. It was a great year for finds! In February, 16-year-old Sierra Sarti-Sweeney found a tooth in Tampa, Florida. And in November, little Kaleb Kidd discovered a mammoth tooth in La Crosse, Wisconsin. At three years old, Kaleb might be the youngest fossil finder ever!

Nature's Memory Keepers

A fossil is the remains of a plant or an animal that lived a long time ago.

The word "fossil" was first used in the 1500s. It comes from a Latin word that means "dug up from the ground." The most common kind of fossil is an imprint, or outline, of the plant or animal in a rock. These kinds of fossils are formed in much the same way as a handprint in clay. Other kinds of fossils include animal bones and footprints, or even a trail left by a worm.

Fossils might be called nature's memory keepers because they show what once was. They are little—or sometimes big—pieces of history. Because fossils give us clues about extinct plants and animals, they help us understand what the world was like in the distant past.

Fossil of a wading bird found in Wyoming

The coastal area where Mary lived was, and still is, full of fossils. Most of these are the remains of animals that lived in the seas between 206 and 144 million years ago, a time known as the Jurassic period. The ichthyosaurus was from this time, when dinosaurs roamed the earth. But Mary was also the first to discover the remains of another Jurassic sea creature.

This skeleton, found in 1823, was equally large and strange. The fossil measured nine feet long and six feet wide. Compared to its giant body, its head was tiny—not quite five inches long! The creature was named Plesiosaurus, meaning "almost like a lizard."

Mary Anning's fossils gave scientists new knowledge about the world.

Mary learned her skills as a fossil hunter from her father. He showed her how to increase the value of her finds by cleaning them with a needle and a small brush, then polishing them. After her father died, Mary's sale of her fossil finds helped keep the family going. Her dedication to this work made her famous as an expert on fossils.

Because she was only a young girl, and not a trained scientist, Mary's knowledge of fossils was almost unbelievable to people of her time. One person wrote that Mary had the knowledge to easily talk with "professors and other clever men on the subject, and they all [admit] she understands more of the science than anyone else in the kingdom."

No wonder Mary Anning has been called "the greatest fossilist the world ever knew."

Plesiosaurus fossil

Trapped in Tar!

Walk down a paved black road on a hot summer day and you might find your shoes starting to sink in. That's because high heat makes the road surface soft. If this happens, you are probably walking on asphalt, or tar.

Luckily, you won't sink in very far. But 28,000 years ago, bubbling black asphalt deposits, or tar pits, swallowed up a great many unlucky animals. Possibly thinking they had found water, the mammoths or ground sloths blundered into pits of sticky, gooey tar. Instead of a drink or a bath, a trap held them fast, forever.

These same tar pits still bubble today—in the middle of Los Angeles, California, one of the largest American cities. But what was bad luck for prehistoric animals has meant good luck for paleontologists, scientists who study fossils.

Known as the Rancho La Brea Tar Pits, the bubbling pools of asphalt contain the remains of woolly mammoths, saber-toothed cats, giant sloths, and other now-extinct beasts. This makes the La Brea Tar Pits one of the world's richest sources of fossils.

Lifelike statues at the tar pits make it easy for visitors to imagine a mammoth's deadly dip. ▶

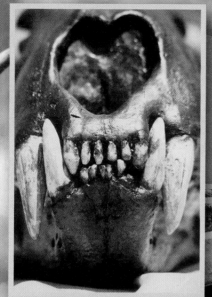

◀ This skull of a saber-toothed cat, from the La Brea Tar Pits, is the only one ever found with its mouth closed.

Paleontologists at work at Los Angeles's Page Museum. ▼

The asphalt in these pits has been oozing from the ground for about 40,000 years, and more than three million fossils have been found. In addition to mammoths, tigers, and sloths, paleontologists have found the remains of horses, coyotes, wolves, bison, birds, rodents, and insects, many in perfect condition.

Today, the La Brea Tar Pits are part of Los Angeles's Page Museum, whose current hot spot is Pit 91. Paleontologists keep finding thousands of fossils in this pit under the watchful eyes of visitors.

After seeing complete animal skeletons and learning how the animals became trapped in tar, a visitor to the Rancho La Brea Tar Pits might feel lucky. Those animals met a fate much worse than leaving a shoe print behind on a black-topped road!

JOURNEY OF THE WOOLLY MAMMOTH

By Maria Fleming

On pillared legs, with tread of thunder,
you trudged across the endless tundra,
a mountain of fur, twin tusks thrust high,
back hunched beneath the weight of the sky.

Until you met some unknown doom,
disappeared into an icy tomb,
a secret buried underground,
ten thousand years lost . . .

Then found.

You walk again inside these walls,
a ghost that haunts museum halls.
Ice Age icon, here enshrined,
once frozen in earth,
now frozen in time.

Prove It!

Half of these statements about fossils are facts. The others are opinions. Take turns reading the statements with a partner. Which are facts (F) and which are opinions (O)?

1. This shell fossil was found in Ithaca, New York.
   o Fact
   o Opinion

2. It would not be a good idea to try to saw petrified wood.
   o Fact
   o Opinion

3. This appears to be the bone of a stegosaurus.
   o Fact
   o Opinion

4. This ammonite fossil shows its coiled shape.
   o Fact
   o Opinion

5. This is the footprint of a terrifying dinosaur.
   o Fact
   o Opinion

6. This fern fossil has four fronds.
   o Fact
   o Opinion

YOUR OPINION COUNTS!

Fairbanks, Alaska

10-year-old Boy Finds 10,000-year-old Tooth!

Newspapers all over the world publish letters from their readers. People often write to offer their opinions about something they've read in the news.

You've read about Jared Post, who found the woolly mammoth tooth in Fairbanks, Alaska. After showing the tooth to scientists, Jared was unsure about whether he would keep it or not.

Suppose you read the story about Jared in a Fairbanks newspaper.

Write a letter to the newspaper telling whether you think Jared should keep the tooth or donate it to a museum—and why you think so. If he keeps the tooth, what should he do with it? If he gives it up, who should get it, and why? Include facts, but focus on your opinion. Explain your reasons for your point of view. If you write a strong, persuasive letter, you might even change someone else's opinion—with help from the tips below.

Tips from the Experts

Do you want to get your letter to the editor published? Here are some pointers.

- **Be Brief.** Get right to the point.
- **Be Accurate.** Check your facts.
- **Be Polite.** Avoid insults.
- **Be Professional.** Remember to sign your letter. Include your name, address, and telephone number. If you e-mail your letter, be sure to include your full name, city, and state.
- **Be Patient.** If at first you don't succeed, keep trying.

Fossil Fish FOUND!

The year was 1938. A strange guest had found its way onboard the *Nerine*, a fishing boat sailing off the coast of South Africa. It was a huge fish with steel-blue eyes and a pale blue body with silver markings. The fishermen had never caught anything like it.

The fish acted strangely, too. It crawled slowly across the boat's deck on fins that looked like stubby legs. It oozed thick oil from its body, and bit the boat captain's hand. Then, about three hours after its capture, it died.

"Old Fourlegs," as the fishermen named it, had no value in the food market. But it was very unusual.

The captain called Marjorie Courtenay-Latimer, who sometimes displayed odd fish in her museum in East London, South Africa.

This was not just any old fish. It was a "living fossil" that caused a worldwide stir. Old Fourlegs turned out to be a *coelacanth* (SEE luh kanth), a fish that first lived about 400 million years ago. Until 1938, scientists had only seen fossils of this kind of fish. They believed it had been extinct for 70 million years!

Coelacanths are sometimes called dinofish because they were around even before dinosaurs.

Unable to identify it, Ms. Courtenay-Latimer wrote to a scientist named J.L.B. Smith. Dr. Smith, an expert on fish, was excited. It sounded to him like the lost coelacanth. By the time he managed to reach East London, the fish had been stuffed and its organs thrown away. Still, he could tell it was a coelacanth.

Dr. Smith spent the next fourteen years looking for another one. He put up posters in places all along Africa's east coast. He offered a cash reward to anyone who found one.

In 1952, Dr. Smith heard that fishermen in the Comoros Islands, near Madagascar, had caught a coelacanth. He rushed to see it and was surprised to learn that the men had caught this kind of fish before, but threw them back in the ocean because they were not good to eat.

Since the discovery of Old Fourlegs, a number of coelacanths have been found, but they are still rare. Many consider this fossil the "most important scientific discovery of the 1900s."

The coelacanth's official name is *Latimeria chalumnae* in honor of Ms. Courtenay-Latimer.

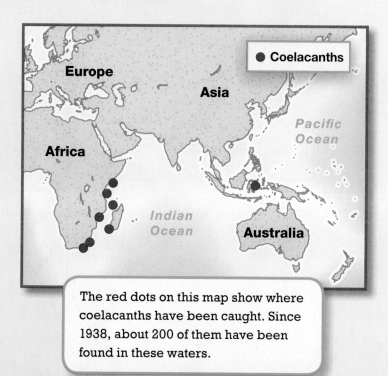

The red dots on this map show where coelacanths have been caught. Since 1938, about 200 of them have been found in these waters.

Fun Fact:
Scientists believe the coelacanth can live up to 100 years.

The Case of the
Missing Deer

"Do you think we'll see some deer soon?" Blake asked.

From their chairs on the small patio, his mom and grandpa both nodded. The three had just arrived at their vacation cabin. Blake was kicking his soccer ball around the wide lawn that their cabin shared with three others. Beyond that were the woods, like a thick green wall. Grandpa had said the deer came right up to the cabins here, and Blake really hoped it was true.

"You'll have to wait until it cools off," Grandpa told him. "But I bet we'll see some this evening."

"Hey, pass me the ball!"

Blake looked up to see a girl about his age coming toward him from the next cabin. He kicked his soccer ball her way.

The girl trapped the ball with her foot. "I'm Maria," she said. "My family has been here three days, and this place is great. But I forgot my soccer ball." She pointed to a third cabin. "There are two brothers staying at that cabin, Nicholas and Todd. We've just been kicking a pinecone around the last couple days."

"I heard that the deer come right up to the cabins around here," Blake said.

"They do. It's really cool."

"All right! A real soccer ball!"

Two boys appeared from around the side of one of the cabins. It was Nicholas and his younger brother, Todd. Within minutes the four of them had a game going, with lawn chairs as goal posts.

The game was loud and rowdy. And even though it was late afternoon, the sun was still strong. Blake pulled his sweatshirt off and flung it on one of the chairs. After an hour of playing, and a few points scored by each team, they wrapped it up.

Maria called to Blake as the new friends all headed back to their own cabins and dinner.

"Hope you see the deer tonight!"

"Me, too!" Blake replied.

But no such luck. After dinner, Blake kept watch for a while at the glass door. When no deer appeared, he joined his family to watch a video. But he kept going to the windows to check. By bedtime, Blake had not caught sight of a single deer. Living in the city, he would never be able to see deer on his doorstep. This was his only chance!

The next day, Blake and his family had a lot of activities planned. But by late afternoon, he caught up again with Maria, Todd, and Nicholas. As they set up pinecones to dribble the soccer ball around, Todd said, "Did you see all the deer last night?"

"A mom and her babies were right outside our kitchen window!" Maria said.

"We didn't see any at all," Blake replied. "We thought maybe it was too cold."

"No way!" Nicholas said. "They were all over the place."

Blake frowned as he kicked the soccer ball across the lawn.

"I'm sure they'll come to your cabin, too, Blake," Maria assured him. "I saw them in your yard before you got here."

"I don't get it," Blake said the next day when he learned his friends had spotted deer in their yards again. Again, the animals had avoided Blake's cabin. What was everyone else doing right?

"Maybe I'll put some food out there. Like some apples," Blake decided. Nicholas, Todd, and Maria thought this might work.

Before dinner, Blake scattered apples near the cabin and all over the yard. He might not catch sight of a deer, but if the apples were eaten, at least he would know they had come to his cabin, too!

The next morning, Blake hurried outside to check on the apples. Not a single bit of apple had been eaten. It looked as if none of them had even been moved.

"It's the case of the missing deer," Todd said when Blake glumly reported his bad news later that afternoon.

"Sounds like a detective story," said Maria.

"One I want to solve!" Blake said. "I need to start thinking like a detective."

"That means starting with all the facts you already know," Nicholas replied.

There were many things the friends knew about the case of the missing deer. They wrote down what cabins the deer went to and when, as well as how many they had seen.

"Are you sure you saw deer around our cabin before we got here?" Blake asked Maria.

She nodded. "Definitely."

"Could it be the soccer ball?" Nicholas asked. "Before you got here, we didn't have one. Maybe the sound bothers the deer."

"But they don't come out at the time of day when we play. At night, it's quiet. So it can't be that."

A search around the cabins provided no clues either. Then Todd had an idea. "Let's check for tracks coming out of the woods!"

Everyone agreed. At the edge of the woods, they found deer tracks heading towards Blake's cabin. But it looked as if the deer had turned back around for some reason.

It was a mystery! The four friends sat down in the screened-in porch at Maria's cabin. As they chatted, Blake picked up a

magazine that sat in a basket near his chair. It had articles about outdoor sports.

As Blake flipped through the pages, one article caught his eye. He read it quickly.

"I've got it!" he said. "I bet I know why the deer have been staying away! Follow me!"

In seconds the friends were standing in Blake's yard, between their lawn-chair goal posts.

"What's the one thing you notice in this yard that isn't in any of the others?" Blake asked.

The three kids looked around. "Just your sweatshirt on the chair," Maria said finally. It had been lying there since their very first soccer game.

"Right!" Blake said. "I just read this article that said deer have a really good sense of smell. It said hunters spray their clothes with something that covers up human scent, because deer run away when they smell people."

"So you think your sweatshirt was keeping the deer away from your yard?" Nicholas asked.

"That's what we're going to find out," Blake said, grabbing his sweatshirt. "Let's see what happens tonight. Everyone come over after dinner."

That evening a soft rustling sounded just beyond Blake's cabin. The four friends were ready and waiting at the sliding glass door. As they watched, two deer and a fawn made their way delicately across the shadowy backyard. They paused to nibble on fresh apples Blake had put out for them.

"You were right!" Maria whispered.

Blake smiled, satisfied at last. "I'd say the case of the missing deer is finally solved!"

Encounter

By Lilian Moore

We both stood
heart-stopping
still,

I in the doorway
the deer
near
the old apple tree,

he
muscle wary
straining
to hear

I holding breath
to say
do not fear.

In the silence
between us
my thought said
Stay!

Did it snap
like a twig?
He rose on a curve
and fled.

Deep in the Forest

By Barbara Juster Esbensen

Deep in the forest
curled in its grassy
bed
the fawn
lies
dappled with circles
lies
hidden under
medallions of sunlight
and woodland gloom
almost invisible

YOU CHOOSE THE ENDING

In "The Case of the Missing Deer," a tossed sweatshirt foreshadows the deer staying away from Blake's cabin. In the story below, events also foreshadow future events. Read to decide which ending makes the most sense—or create your own ending.

THE MISSING REPORT MYSTERY

It was Laura's birthday, but she wasn't happy. All weekend she had worked hard on a science report about woodland habitats. Now it was missing.

"It's the best report I've ever written," Laura moaned, looking down at her family's new puppy.

"Come with me, Rusty," she said. "Let's look for my report." Rusty wagged his tail and dropped the newspaper he'd been chewing on.

Laura led Rusty from room to room.

"Have you seen my report?" Laura asked her sister Paige, who was sitting at the kitchen table. Paige quickly slid something under a placemat.

"Report?" she asked. "What report?"

Ending 1: Laura finds her report in the living room, chewed to pieces by Rusty. Paige had been making a surprise birthday card for Laura.

Ending 2: Rusty leads Laura to the report, which he had carried in his mouth to her school.

Ending 3: Paige hid Laura's report, so she could surprise her by making a drawing for its cover.

WHO DID IT?

After reading "Fossil Fish Found!," you know that a few people were involved in the 1938 discovery of the coelacanth. The main ones were:

A. Dr. Smith

B. Ms. Courtenay-Latimer

C. The captain of the *Nerine* fishing boat

Read each of the six statements below. Which person above does each statement best correspond to? On a separate sheet of paper, match each statement to a person by writing the number and letter that go together.

1. First to see the strange fish

2. Thought the fish might be a coelacanth

3. First to contact Dr. Smith about the fish

4. Offered a reward for more coelacanths

5. Was bitten by the strange fish

6. Had the strange fish stuffed

For centuries people have been writing down their experiences in diaries and journals. Journals have opened a window on what life was like in many different times and places.

A journal entry can be a good way to help you write a personal narrative about an experience. For example, in "The Case of the Missing Deer," Blake might have written about his excitement at seeing the doe and fawn.

Write your own personal narrative. Think about a discovery you have made, and write a journal entry about it. It can be a place you have visited, something you've done for the first time, or something you've observed in nature. It can also be a fictional discovery—a place you imagine seeing or an activity you imagine doing.

Write the date for your journal entry. Record your thoughts, feelings, and what you saw, heard, and did on this particular day. Include details! Write so that someone reading your journal will understand something about you and the world you are writing about. If you like, include small drawings that relate to your writing.

May 25

Today was a momentous
day. I saw a bald eagle
for the first time.
It was perched in
a tree at the
edge of
the lake.

Journey to Cuzco:

The Origin of the Inca

The Incan empire of South America was once the largest empire in the Americas. It stretched through the Andes mountain range from present-day Colombia to Chile. The Inca's great skill in farming and building can be seen in the ruins of Machu Picchu (MAH choo PEE choo), near Cuzco (KOOS koh), Peru.

The following ancient myth tells about the origin of the Incan civilization.

Machu Picchu lies on a mountain ridge about 8,000 feet high.

Clone out TX box

TK

Viracuchu (veer uh KOO choo), the sky god, saw that the night sky was empty. So he created the moon, the stars, and the planets.

Viracuchu's son was Inti (IHN tee), the god of the sun. Inti felt that people needed order in their lives. On a lake in the Andes, he created the first Incan people. They were Manco Capac (MAHN koh KAH pahk) and his sister, Mama Ocllo (MAH mah OHK yo). Inti sent them on a journey. Their mission was to find the place for the Incan civilization to begin.

How would Manco Capac and Mama Ocllo know when they had found the right spot? Inti had given them a golden staff. The chosen place would be where the staff sank deep into the earth.

The brother and sister journeyed into the bitterly cold Andes Mountains. They traveled through underground caves. At times they discovered hidden valleys. At each location, they tested the ground. It was always too hard; the golden staff would not go through.

Finally, the travelers came upon the most beautiful valley they had seen. When they tried the staff, it went so deep into the earth that it disappeared. They knew they had arrived. The site became Cuzco, the first capital of the Incan empire.

Manco Capac and Mama Ocllo taught men and women to farm and build houses, to weave cloth and to prepare food. From these humble beginnings, the great civilization of the Inca developed, with Manco Capac as its first emperor.

Manco Capac

After you read the myth, describe how it explains the origins of people, places, and phenomena in nature.

Get Lost!
The Puzzle of Mazes

Getting through a maze can be a challenge!

Imagine you are running along a narrow, gravel pathway. On either side of you is a six-foot wall of tangled hedges. Openings along the hedge lead to other long, leafy green hallways. They all look the same. You are caught in a maze! Can you find your way out? Even a compass won't help you. Many of these twisting passageways will never take you to the end. Instead, they lead to dead ends and you have to retrace your steps. This is what makes mazes so much fun—and so difficult!

What's a Labyrinth?

Many people confuse mazes with labyrinths. Unlike mazes, many labyrinths have no walls at all. They are simply designs built into a floor or other flat surface. Mazes are multicursal, meaning they have many paths. A labyrinth is unicursal—it has a single path from the beginning to the end. Most labyrinths are less challenging than mazes, but there's one exception you'll read about on page 73!

Hemmed In by Hedges

Hedge mazes are one of the most common kinds of mazes. These are often made from the yew, an evergreen tree or shrub. Yews make good maze borders because they grow slowly and keep their shape.

Mazes are created in all kinds of designs from easy to difficult. Some mazes end in their middle. In others, you must find your way from one side to another. In 1977, Queen Elizabeth celebrated twenty-five years as queen of England. To mark this event, brothers Edward and Lindsay Heyes created the Silver Jubilee maze.

The slow-growing yew tree

This "aMazing Hedge Puzzle," as the brothers call it, has twelve paths to the center and thirteen unlucky dead ends. And there's a balcony outside the maze from which you can shout hints to your friends inside—or confuse them even more!

The Silver Jubilee maze pathways can hold many people at once, and even wheelchairs. So many people visit that the paths wear down two inches a year!

The length of mazes can vary, too. Some are extremely long. In 1975, for example, Greg Bright created the Longleat Hedge Maze in Wiltshire, England. This maze, one of the longest hedge mazes in the world, uses more than 16,000 English yew trees. It takes about ninety minutes to complete. Other mazes are short and may take very little time to finish.

The Longleat Hedge Maze has almost two miles of pathways.

A Royal Puzzle

One of the most unusual hedge mazes is found at Leeds Castle in Kent, England. Made from yew and designed by a maze expert, it was planted in 1988. Part of the maze is cut in the shape of a crown to honor the many queens who have lived in the castle. At the center of the Leeds Castle maze is the entrance to a grotto, or cavern, filled with sculptures of mythical beasts.

The maze at Leeds Castle in Kent, England

If you're lucky enough to find your way to the center, you can climb to the top of a small tower for a view of the entire maze. Then you can take stone steps down into the most unique part of the maze—its grotto. The maze winds through an underground cave that's cold, dark, and narrow. This part of the maze is unicursal, which means it has a single path leading from the beginning to the end. You can't get lost!

Can you find the crown in the maze?

If you find your way to the center tower, you will have the chance to explore the underground part of the Leeds maze.

For younger children, Leeds Castle offers the Turf Maze. No taller than ankle height, this maze also has a surprise at its center—a small wooden castle. Leeds Castle offers something to amaze both the young and the old.

Even young children enjoy the maze experience at Leeds Castle.

Underground you will pass a fountain carved in the shape of a mysterious face. Follow the light to the end of the maze!

Lost in the Cornstalks

There are hedge mazes in the United States, but not as many as in England. Our most common type of maze is made from cornstalks. It's nicknamed a maize maze because maize is another word for corn.

Unlike hedge mazes, which last for years, maize mazes last for only one season. However, they are fast and easy to grow. Designs are usually cut into the cornfield with tractors when the corn is only a few inches high. Picture designs are especially popular for maize mazes. And since corn is tallest in the fall, these designs are often related to the season of autumn.

Maize mazes are fun but hot and dusty inside. Be sure to bring water and wear running shoes instead of sandals when you try one!

Not all maize mazes have autumn themes. In 1993 British maze designer Adrian Fisher created a huge corn maze in the shape of a dinosaur in Harrisburg, Pennsylvania. Other maize mazes have featured castles, a map of the United States, an Egyptian pyramid, the Statue of Liberty, a cowboy, a pig, and even a portrait of the actor John Wayne.

Corn mazes are created in all kinds of imaginative designs!

A Test of Skill

Have you ever tried making your way through a maze on paper? If so, you know you place your pencil at "Start" and draw a line all the way through to the end. If you practice solving paper mazes, it might help you find your way through a hedge or maize maze. You may not need to go very far to try. Mazes have become popular tourist attractions, and they're found all over the world. Maybe you'll get a chance to test your maze-solving skills outdoors. Good luck!

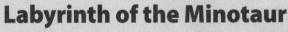

Labyrinth of the Minotaur

A story from Greek mythology has made one labyrinth famous the world over. In ancient days, King Minos ruled the island of Crete where people lived in fear of a beast called the Minotaur. The Minotaur had the head of a bull and the body of a man.

Minos kept the Minotaur in a huge labyrinth. Every few years fourteen people were sacrificed to the Minotaur. But Theseus, a brave young man, volunteered to stop this terrible practice by battling the Minotaur.

King Minos' daughter, Ariadne, gave Theseus a sword to fight the Minotaur and a ball of string to help him find his way out of the labyrinth. Theseus killed the Minotaur, rescued the people who were meant to be victims, and led them out to freedom.

"Minotaur Waking," a bronze sculpture by Michael Ayrton

Poetry Place

The Best Paths

by Kristine O'Connell George

The best paths
are whispers
in the grass,
a bent twig,
a token, a hint,
easily missed.

The best paths
hide themselves
until the right
someone
comes along.

The best paths
lead you
to where
you didn't know
you wanted to go.

compass

by Valerie Worth

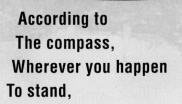

According to
The compass,
Wherever you happen
To stand,

North, south,
East and west,
Meet in the palm
Of your hand.

MEMORY MAZE

Grand Opening

MAY'S MAZES

DISCOVER THE TIGER HEDGE MAZE!

- Find your way to the giant tiger in the center!
- Twenty dead ends and only one right path!

STROLL THE LAKESIDE LABYRINTH!

- Music from hidden speakers!
- Dancing fountains!

TRY MAY'S MAIZE MAZE!

- Cornstalks twelve feet tall!
- Clue sheets for the confused!

Read the above ad. Discuss with a partner how it presents its message differently than an online ad or a TV commercial might. Then test your memory. Cover the ad and read the list of details on the right. Tell which maze each one goes with.

Twenty dead ends!	_____?_____
Dancing fountains!	_____?_____
Clue sheets!	_____?_____
Hidden speakers!	_____?_____
Giant tiger!	_____?_____
Cornstalks!	_____?_____

A-maze Yourself!

You don't need a cornfield or hedge paths to make a maze. Here are instructions to help you make your own maze at home or in class.

Materials:

Pencil, paper, and eraser

Step 1 Draw a large rectangle for the frame of the maze. Use the diagram on this page as a guide. Mark where you want your maze to start (S) and finish (F).

Step 2 Start making your paths. Make horizontal lines and vertical lines to turn your path in different directions. Put a line across your path to make a dead end.

Step 3 After you have finished your maze, try to solve it. You may need to close off some paths or open others.

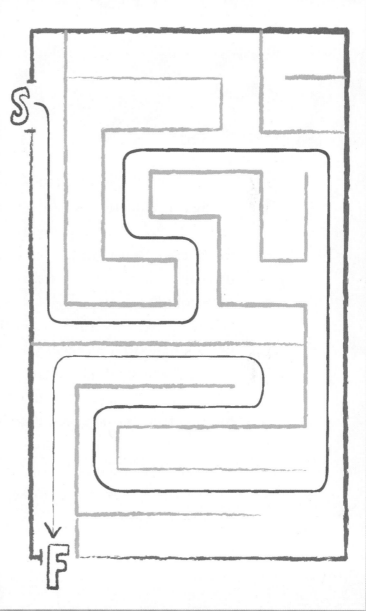

Extras

- Make your maze in the shape of an object or animal.

- Draw little pictures or write messages by the paths.

A Writer's TREASURE

A treasure is waiting to be found, but only you know where it is hidden! How can you help someone find it? First, on a separate sheet of paper, write a sentence that tells what the treasure is and where the seeker needs to go. (It could be anywhere—in a Chinese forest, a fictional island, or in your own house.)

Next, write instructions for finding the treasure. Is it buried underground, tucked in a hollow log, or hidden in an attic? Wherever it is, choose a starting point and write step-by-step instructions that will lead someone to the hiding place. Include clear details—landmarks and site markers—in your instructions. Add a few directions that will require using a compass, too.

Finally, you can also draw a simple map to go with the instructions.

Here is an example.

MAP

Treasure Oak

Village of
Coolhead

Fern
Hill

Fern Park

Island of Bells

Village of
Hot Foot

N

W

E

S

The treasure is three golden coins.

You will need to travel to the Island of Bells.

1. Go to Fern Park in the village of Coolhead.

2. Walk to the twisted oak tree. Look in the hollow for a key.

3. Walk east for 45 steps.

4. Look for a blue rock.

5. Dig under the rock exactly three feet.

6. Find the green metal box and use the key!

Credits